DATE DUE

NO 30 90			
JA 7 9			
9 8			
OC 14 98			
NO 16 98			
OC 19 99			

RIVERSIDE COMMUNITY COLLEGE
LIBRARY
Riverside, California

EVERYONE CAN WIN

Every person has a potential for talent
a capacity for creativity
and a right to enjoy to the fullest
the beauty and vitality of the arts.

JEAN KENNEDY SMITH

Founder
Very Special Arts

OPPORTUNITIES AND PROGRAMS
IN THE ARTS FOR THE DISABLED

EVERY-ONE CAN WIN

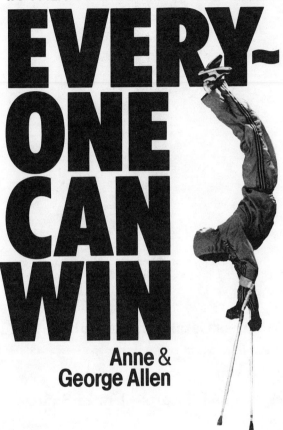

**Anne &
George Allen**

*For everyone who has ever helped
a disabled person to achieve
the validation of the grandeur of the
human spirit
that is the creative artistic act*

Library of Congress Cataloging-in-Publication Data

Allen, Anne.
    Everyone can win.

    1. Handicapped and the arts—United States.
I. Allen, George. II. Title.
NX180.H34A45   1988   700′.880816   88-1193
ISBN 0-939009-09-9

EPM Publications, Inc., 1003 Turkey Run Road,
    McLean, Virginia 22101

Printed in the United States of America

Cover and book design by Tom Huestis
Cover photograph is of Eddie Fernandez,
    break dancer

CONTENTS

FOREWORD

The sending and receiving of sophisticated messages gives human beings a special identity and meaning and sets us apart from all other creatures on the planet Earth. Like other forms of life, we build our nests; we seek our mates; and we flee from or confront our enemies. But unlike others, we take infinite pains to express and record our feelings and ideas. We capture those experiences through the miracle we call language.

In the early dawn of civilization, our ancestors used sticks and stones and grunts and groans to convey feelings and ideas. Words were formed. A vocabulary took shape, followed by written symbols, making it possible to send messages from place to place and to transmit them from one generation to another. Poets shaped metaphors, forcing us to view familiar things in unfamiliar ways, while the rhythm of words carried yet another kind of meaning.

But even with the beauty and the power of the written and the spoken word, our miraculous use of language was incomplete. There remained buried in the bosom of the human spirit those human experiences that could not be captured by the sounds and verbal impressions we call words. These symbols simply could not fully portray such joy as the coming of spring or the fruits of a fall harvest or the grief and loneliness that marked the ending of a love. They could not adequately convey the sound of the brook or the setting of the evening sun.

For the most intimate, most profoundly moving universal experiences we need a more subtle, more sensitive set of symbols than the written and the spoken word. This richer language we call the arts. And so it is that men and women have used music, dance, and the visual arts to transmit our human heritage most effectively and to express most profoundly our deepest joys, sorrows, and intuitions.

There is only one incontrovertible conclusion to be reached. The arts are not a frill; they are an essential part of language, and this is the theme underlying *Everyone Can Win*. In this powerfully persuasive and deeply moving book the Allens remind us just how deeply the arts give meaning to those with special disabilities. For years I have chaired a national committee concerned with the arts for the handicapped, now called Very Special Arts, precisely because I feel children who are visually or mentally impaired or physically restricted should have other means to convey feelings and ideas. We all know of the acuteness of hearing of the visually impaired, just as the deaf can "see" more because they must rely so much on vision. Deprived of the capacity to convey feelings and ideas through one sense, they turn to another: to visual language or to music, dance or the canvas.

Everyone Can Win demonstrates that the arts have a powerful potential. In this work, beautiful stories are told by piecing together the extraordinary ways the handicapped can pursue and enjoy the arts, thereby enriching their own lives and those of others. Never has the message been stronger: not only do the arts fulfill our culture, they help those who are disabled to convey feelings and ideas and to release imprisoned emotions.

The incredible "democracy" of the arts, their ability to represent and accommodate us all, whatever our limitations, has never been made quite so clear as in this extremely valuable report by Anne and George Allen. *Everyone Can Win*, while inspirational for the general reader, serves as a first-class primer for those in our schools and colleges who should be finding ways to extend the arts beyond the curriculum slots into which they are all too often placed.

After visiting countless classrooms and lecture halls, I am convinced that all students at all levels urgently need to see connections. And I believe that finding patterns across the separate disciplines can be accomplished through the arts. Albert Einstein wrote on one occasion that religions, arts, and sciences are branches of the same tree. What the Allens make indisputably clear in this book is that these branches are even more vital to the lives of the handicapped.

ERNEST L. BOYER

President
The Carnegie Foundation for the
Advancement of Teaching

Chairman of the Board
Very Special Arts

CHAPTER ONE

Art Benefits Disabled People A New Idea

*Only through art can we get
outside of ourselves
and know another's view of
the universe
and see landscapes
which otherwise would have
remained unknown to us.*

— MARCEL PROUST

If you have a disability, learning to practice an art will bring you enormous benefits. Which disability you have and which art form you choose doesn't matter, the benefits are bound to come.

If you are not disabled you need to understand the truth—and the importance—of this proposition, particularly if you are a relative, teacher, therapist, counselor or friend of someone who has a handicap.

For some people who have limitations, art may be the *major* means of expression they have. And no matter how well they can communicate otherwise, art increases the opportunities and the range available to them for liberating self-expression. As a result they are better able to reach others who have impairments as well as the "normals" with whom they work and socialize. The production of works which are appreci-

11

ated by others increases the artists' feelings of self-worth by proving to them that they, too, are achievers.

The idea that the arts could be enriching and beneficial for disabled people entered very few heads until quite recently. Only 10 years ago, as part of an effort to get federal funding for an arts program, Phyllis Wyeth, wife of painter Jamie Wyeth, had to make this elementary explanation to the United States Congress: "The arts may be the handicapped person's first chance for achieving a goal, his first step toward success in other areas of learning, the first sign that his life will have meaning and significance."

The need for Ms. Wyeth to spell out the basics of the concept for the Congress as late as 1977 reveals how new it is. Among activities for the disabled, the oldest and best known is physical therapy, which is in the field of medicine. Physical therapy's nonmedical adjunct, organized sports for the disabled, have long since proved their value and are well known. The benefits of participation in the arts, on the other hand, are little known among the estimated 35 million disabled Americans and the 60 or 70 million parents, siblings, spouses, physicians, therapists, counselors, teachers and friends who are influential in their lives. Developmental disability, which affects about 40 percent of our disabled population is the most widespread handicap. An important step forward for everyone concerned with handicaps has been the dawning realization that when it comes to creative potential,

Sani Inches and Lewis Merkin in a scene from the National Theatre of the Deaf's production of The Dybbuk: Between Two Worlds, *presented in sign language and the spoken word.* Sally Andersen-Bruce

particularly in the nonverbal arts, *there is no difference* between those who are developmentally retarded and the rest of the world's population.

The general recognition of the many values the arts have for disabled people began only about 20 years ago. And only during the past decade has there been a systematic effort to mount the educational and teaching programs needed to bring the benefits of the arts to the one in eleven Americans who are disabled. Now the field is exploding. There are art programs for handicapped people operating, or being formed, in all 50 states and in 40 other countries. The first international seminar on the subject was held in Washington in May 1984.

"What art, any art, can do is help all individuals find their *own* centers—who they *really* are—before everybody tells them who they should be," is the way Bob Alexander summed up the art experience. He has been helping physically and mentally limited children for more than 20 years as director of Living Stage. "What happens with these kids is that they start to believe, to accept, that in their lives, using their imaginations is a valid first step, an important second step and an essential third step. It validates who they really are before they become what society would make them."

The experiences people gain from art are sometimes so fantastic that parents, friends, physicians and particularly teachers have difficulty believing them. One of the purposes of this book is to document the stories of such experiences. You will read about a blind girl who had not spoken for seven years but who talked imaginatively and at length after her first art experience. Another girl, an adolescent described as a "vegetable" by her teachers—she could not speak or stand—helped write a poem during her first artistic

14

experience and then, as the poem was read aloud, interpreted it with dance movements as she lay on the floor.

The heads-up, best-foot-forward attitude that art experiences can develop in the disabled was well expressed by a member of the National Theatre of the Deaf: "We are not six-cylinder cars operating on only five cylinders. We are five-cylinder cars sure working on every one of them."

"Being disabled reduces what I can do," says another artist, "but makes me more determined to get recognition for the work. I'm not going through this world quietly."

The latter artist has the use of two hands. What of someone who has neither arms nor hands but aspires to both art and independence? Neita Kemmel was born without either hands or arms. This is how she describes her experience: "People used to look at me and say, 'poor thing, she can't do anything.' But one day something happened. The little girl who couldn't do anything was painting by holding the brush in her mouth." Today Neita earns her living from her art.

Observers like physicians, teachers and family members often notice that when a disabled person takes up art it has a measurable therapeutic effect on their emotions, on their psyches, even on their physical abilities. And many such observers hold that for disabled people the primary value of art is as therapy. Indeed, built upon that perception—and art's undeniable values—a respected and widespread profession of art therapy has grown up. However, the use of art as therapy generates controversy and we feel we should make clear where we stand on the matter.

We are not promoting nor discussing art as therapy. Art therapy is a branch of medicine. The aim of therapy is to help people live their lives with reduced anxiety, pain and anguish. Therapy has little or nothing to do with the creative part of the human being. We believe that a disabled person should enter into art for exactly the same reasons that anyone else does. They should do so for fun, joy, creation, expression, or to fulfill some deep-seated desire or drive. There is no difference between art for people who have handicaps and for those who don't. We believe art should very rarely be entered into for therapy. There is something of a paradox involved here. It is demonstrably true that when the *intent* is not therapy, the effect of art will have a greater therapeutic effect. But this book is not about therapy. It is about creativity.

The importance of creativity was well set forth by two pioneers in the movement to provide the benefits art brings to people with disabilities. They are Florence Ludins-Katz and her husband, Elias Katz, a psychologist, who live in California. In their 1987 book *Freedom to Create*, written for teachers, they write about children, but their perceptions apply equally to people of any age. In their introduction to the work they say this:

"Why is it so important that disabled children be encouraged to express their creativity? Disabled children for so long have mistakenly been characterized as incapable of producing anything but poor or mediocre art. When given the chance and encouragement, surprising results occur.

"We believe that all people are creative, but unfortunately encouragement of creativity has been limited to the few with 'special talent.' There is absolutely no way of judging 'special talent' if the person has not been encouraged to make use of the creativity that lies within him.

"A school environment in which creativity is appreciated, stimulated, and encouraged opens up to the children whole new areas of expression and imagination. They are able to put down what they feel, what they think, how they react to the world around them and how the world reacts to them.

"Creativity is never measured; no grades are given; nor is it compared with the creativity of other students. Here is a chance to dream, to explore, to let out emotions, to feel equal with all people, and perhaps even superior, because you have a secret which can be shared with those who understand you. But this emotional outlet is only one need in the classroom that is met by creative work. The release of creativity through the arts enters all fields of education. It teaches the student how to think creatively in all school subjects; how to make judgments; how to complete a task, and the satisfaction that comes with the completion of the task.

" 'To quote Dr. Elliot Eisner, Professor of Education and Art at Stanford University:

" 'Artistic tasks, unlike so much of what is now taught in schools, develop the ability to judge, to assess, to experience a range of meanings that exceed what we are able to say in words. The limits of language are not the limits of our consciousness. The arts, more than any other areas of human endeavor, exploit this human capacity.' "

Melville Appell, who is with the Special Education Program of the federal government's Department of Education, sees even more happening when a disabled person gets into one of the arts:

"An armless artist who paints a lovely picture while holding the brush in her teeth or between her toes will be regarded as something quite dramatic, while the artist herself experiences the act of creation as something highly emotionally fulfilling. But there's even more: the act of creation of art means that a life is

17

being fulfilled; not the life of a disabled person as distinct from a nondisabled person, but the fulfillment of the life of a person, *any* person. The aspiration to artistic endeavor increases the beauty and quality of life for *everyone*, disabled or not. When practicing one of the arts and reaping the benefits of that practice, there is absolutely no difference between the disabled and nondisabled."

Developmentally handicapped people may gain benefits from the arts they can find nowhere else. Explains Jack Kreitzer, a poet who works with disabled children and adults in South Dakota:

"For those with mental difficulties, the arts are a way to integrate internal and external realities, particularly since the level of intelligence and the degree of creativity are not directly related. The visual arts can be a means to transmit an emotional truth that may be too difficult to verbalize. Thus the arts become vehicles for self-awareness. In art people who have disabilities can dare to go beyond normalization, to strive for and savor excellence and dignity."

Even when it comes to the down-to-earth, practical, everyday nitty gritty of life for the developmentally delayed, the arts have benefits. Says Jacqueline Merritt, Director of the VSA program for the state of Iowa:

"The arts are a good way to teach those who have mental limitations many practical things. I'm talking about being able to talk better because you have been in a singing group, about being able to hold your shoulders back, being able to remember which is your right foot and which is your left and being able to walk better because you have been learning to dance and being able to work in a group because you were part of a drama production."

The main goal for disabled practitioners of the arts—or at least for the vast majority of them—is not

18

to produce great art, nor even acceptable art, but to enjoy themselves, widen their horizons and to mix with others, ending their isolation—often self-imposed—from the main stream of society. To engage in an art, the disabled person must learn about it from others, study with them, practice with them, and often perform with them. In performing, as with dancing and music, or showing, as with painting and poetry, you *communicate* with others. Whether your audience is strangers or people you know, you communicate to an extent and in a style that you could never achieve any other way.

Dr. Vivienne Anderson, a former Associate Commissioner of Education for New York State and a founding member of Very Special Arts, who is now on the VSA board of directors, emphasized for us that when disabled persons take up an art form it is hard to overestimate the chances that the venture will improve their lives:

"Participation in an art form helps disabled people to get over that horrendous sense of isolation they have—an isolation it is difficult for those of us who are not disabled to understand. To come out of that isolation, to begin to relate openly with others with increasing security and greater happiness is a tremendous asset."

That the arts have special values for children and young people is a view held by Dr. Lawrence Riccio, Director of Washington Very Special Arts, who teaches teachers how to use art in their classrooms:

"For young people, the arts are great levelers, great equalizers. When you know how to do an art, that tells people you've got neat skills. You may be mentally retarded or have a physical disability that requires you to use a wheelchair, but if you can get up on a stage and sing or play an instrument or read poetry or paint with your mouth, people say to each other, 'Hey, this person has talent, that's neat.' Yes, it is neat, and it's very neat for young artists—makes them feel great, makes them feel equal."

Some may wonder if there really ever could be genuine equality between the disabled and nondisabled in any field. Well, in some sports, people with handicaps do achieve equality and that achievement can be quite dramatic. Anne saw this when she visited the marvelous skiing program for the disabled run by Hal O'Leary in Winter Park, Colorado, in the Rocky Mountains not far from Denver.

"Winter Park is at the ten-thousand foot level and the air is thin," she wrote. "When I got there, just walking a few steps winded me and I had to sit down. Hal O'Leary sat beside me and pointed up the mountain. I aimed my binoculars and saw a half-dozen fast and wonderfully graceful skiers schussing down toward us. It wasn't until they ended their run close in front of us that I could see each skier was using only one ski—each was missing a leg. But on that slope they were every bit as fast and as graceful as two-legged skiers; there was no difference between them."

Of his famed program, in which disabled skiers use the same slopes as the nondisabled, Mr. O'Leary tells: "We operate in the belief that participation in sports with the general population shatters myths about the handicapped. When you see a one-legged skier whipping past you on the slopes, you are suddenly confronted in a very direct way—not with that person's disabilities—but with their abilities."

You may be convinced that art is the thing, but nevertheless feel that some kinds of disabilities preclude participating in it. If, for example, you can manage only the most limited movement, you may feel that art is not for you. That might have been true as recently as five years ago, but not today with the help of the newest computers. Though computers have been oversold in some markets, they certainly are of enormous value to creative people and people with physical limitations. A computer has enabled us as writers to double our output of words with much less fatigue than with an electric typewriter; by doing so it has enlarged our time to think and consequently enlarged our ability to create. The same is true for people with disabilities. Computers can enlarge their scope physically, intellectually and creatively.

Almost every week a new piece of computer equipment comes on the market which makes these electronic wonders more useful to an ever-growing number of handicapped persons. The advancements are coming at such a rate that to cover them adequately would require a separate book. Here we can present only the briefest of indications of the marvelous aids that are available.

For writers and poets who are blind there is, for example, the "Versabraille," a portable typewriter-like machine that stores Braille from the keyboard on a cassette, which in turn permits the work to be edited before it is printed. The editing is accomplished by moving pins which form Braille characters in much the same way that the pins of dot matrix computer printers form the letters of the English alphabet. The "Versabraille" pins can be read by the fingertips like traditional Braille. After editing, the machine not only prints out a Braille manuscript, but it also translates the Braille text into standard English and prints that. Blind students use the little computer to write their papers and essays in Braille for themselves and simultaneously in English for their teachers.

For the visual artist there is an electronic drawing board that attaches to a computer. The artist draws with one or two fingers on the board and the computer screen reproduces the figure. Some Braille printers now can reproduce free-form drawings precisely in raised dots.

For the blind who can hear, there are systems in which the computer pronounces each letter or each word as it is entered on the keyboard. Far from the early days when synthesized speech sounded as though it came from a robot and was barely intelligible, the new synthesized voices have come a long way. At a computer show we listened to a synthesized voice of a woman that was barely distinguishable from normal speech.

For the person whose hand and finger movements are extremely limited, almost any computer can be rigged to respond to two switches that can be operated by one finger with minimal movement and pressure. One switch is set on the left, the other on the right, within the range of motion of one finger. One switch generates dots and the other, dashes and the computer is programmed to read Morse code, which it translates into letters and words. If a person can't move a finger well enough for this system, the same results can be achieved with puffs of air from his mouth.

These days if you can blink your eye, you can control a computer. This seemingly impossible feat is accomplished by means of a tiny electronic generator attached to an eyeglass frame worn by the operator. The generator emits an infrared beam to which the computer is programmed to respond. Blinking an eye interrupts the beam and the computer can read the interruptions and interpret them as instructions.

The newly heightened visibility of people with handicaps and their moves into the mainstream of society, however slow, have brought confusion in the choice of words used to describe them. The word "crippled" went

Jamie Wyeth admires the work of students participating in a Very Special Arts workshop.

by the board more than a decade ago, and rightly so. Over the years it had taken on a pejorative meaning. But the euphemisms that have sprung up to replace it are not much better. The two that have crossed our horizon most frequently are "differently abled" and "physically challenged." People who use these terms do so with good intent; they are trying to convey the message: "I'm concerned with your strengths, not your weaknesses. I'm seeing you, not your wheelchair." However, in trying to show good will and wanting to find a mild name for something disagreeable, they become prudish and overdelicate. They remind us of the Victorians who, in an age when it was impolite even to hint at sexual matters, called legs limbs and some-

23

times covered piano legs with ruffled bloomers. We prefer language that is clear and direct. To us a spade is a spade, and the disabled are disabled.

It may surprise some people to learn that disabled people do not universally appreciate the use of euphemisms. A fairly large proportion of those we have interviewed find the euphemisms unacceptable. Disabled people, of course, are those most qualified to speak to the issue. Sculptor Sanda Aronson of New York City is especially articulate on the subject. She has severe allergies that keep her housebound and also an undiagnosed muscular condition that requires her to use a wheelchair. This is what she told us:

"I hate euphemisms for 'disabled.' They confuse the hell out of people as well as seeming to me like Band-Aids or 'make it nice.' Most of [the disabled people I deal with] hate them too: 'differently-abled,' 'physically challenged,' etc. I remember being confused for years about what 'differently abled' and 'developmentally disabled' was, the latter being a euphemism for retarded.

"I hate being different physically. My art process is the same as every artist's creative process. I am not 'differently-abled.'

". . .So often disabled people are called 'brave' by a well- meaning press and well-meaning friends. It's not in what we are called, but *how we are perceived.* [emphasis added] We are not 'brave' for going about our lives, making the best of every day and doing things like going to school, making art, some of us earning a living, marrying, etc.

"Some of us *are* brave, but it isn't because of our doing the things able-bodied people do. That is where they often see us crookedly. The problem is that TV and the general population see us as different, strange, weird, odd. Once we are perceived as others are, just

24

physically or mentally different, we are then seen as people.

"One job for a disabled person is more valuable—and much more appreciated—than a thousand euphemisms."

As far as many—perhaps most—disabled people are concerned, actions speak a good deal louder than words. Actions are what this book is all about—actions by teachers, artists and other leaders who have opened new vistas for the disabled and actions by the disabled themselves who have gained new self-confidence through self-expression and inspired others like themselves to venture forth into the beckoning, promising fields of the arts.

CHAPTER TWO

Dance I
Silent Poetry

Dancing is the loftiest,
the most moving,
the most beautiful of the arts,
because it is no mere translation
or abstraction from life;
it is life itself.

—HAVELOCK ELLIS, The Dance of Life

We begin with dance because dance is the art most concerned with movement; and for the disabled—those who are blind or deaf as well as those who have disabilities that inhibit the action of their limbs—ease of movement, grace of movement, expansion of movement is counted among the most pervasive of problems. Dance also deserves pride of place for it is the most intimate, the most moving, the most life-affecting—particularly for the disabled—of the arts since the stuff of which it is made is ourselves, our bodies and our psyches. We'll begin our treatise on dance with the accomplishments of those who are deaf because they, as a group, have made the most spectacular advances in using dance as a way to destroy the ster-

Carol Penn, founder and director of New Visions Dance Theatre in the District of Columbia, is using patterning to teach Ronald Wells, 12, who is blind, how to plié.

Ozier Muhammad

eotype that to be disabled also means to be incapable, a perception that is rampant in much of the world.

There are about two million deaf people in the U.S. and around another 14 million hear very poorly. Most people who were born deaf or became deaf very early in life cannot form the sounds of speech well enough to be understood. It is this circumstance which gave rise to the ancient canard "deaf and dumb." And, inevitably, in popular but uninformed belief, the second term of the absurdity was understood to mean ignorant or stupid. Even at this late date in the supposedly modern twentieth century, those who are deaf still must ceaselessly remind the hearing world that *deaf* does not also mean *dumb*. And one of the best ways to proclaim this is through the performing arts.

Many deaf people will tell you that if they had to choose between disabilities they would choose blindness over deafness. The reason for such a Draconian choice? The deaf point out that their disability is the most isolating. People who are blind or who have other disabilities can hear music and speech, can hear the sound of approaching danger like an automobile or truck, can communicate more or less normally with others and can attend classes with the main stream of students.

A communications barrier separates the world of the profoundly deaf and the world of the hearing that is in most circumstances greater than that of almost any other disability. About a quarter million of them either were born deaf or lost their hearing in the first two or three years of life. These are the people who have the greatest communication barrier. Before he can talk, a baby's brain stores the sounds of speech it hears for later use as a basis for learning language. If the child is deprived of those early years of acquiring the basis for language, the loss can never be made up. For them,

28

trying to learn the elements of English is like trying to put up a building without blueprints or without understanding how tools work.

To most people who can hear, deafness seems a simple, straightforward disability without hidden dimensions. They believe deaf persons can read newspapers and books, can communicate through writing notes and reading lips. But deafness for those who were deaf early in life is more complex. To write a sentence that is correctly structured is for someone who never has heard the sounds of speech a Herculean task. To read a newspaper probably is difficult and to read a book of any weight can be close to impossible. As far as dealing with the written language is concerned, very many deaf people are in the same boat as those who are severely learning disabled. The hearing world also greatly overrates the usefulness of lip reading. Because vowels are formed in the back of the mouth many English words look precisely the same on the lips. In front of a mirror try, for instance, "hat," "hit," and "hot." The best deaf lip readers may get perhaps 30 percent of what is said. For the rest, they make guesses based on the context. Most deaf lip readers don't understand anywhere near 30 percent of a conversation.

Barriers to communication, no matter where they are encountered, nearly always create prejudice. Because of the prejudice of many hearing people against the deaf, as recently as 20 years ago some landlords were refusing to rent houses to deaf people. In her book *A Loss for Words: The Story of Deafness in a Family*, Lou Ann Walker, the hearing daughter of deaf parents, reports that a mechanic once refused to repair the family's car because it was owned by deaf people. Her family's greatest problems were due to hearing people failing to understand them. Others gave them either too little or too much solicitude. Her parents were frequently embarrassed in public when people stared at the sound of their voices or at their signing. Ms. Walker writes that she grew up with the "odd, inescapable feeling that society thought it was some kind of sin to be deaf."

The unyielding nature of the barrier to communication between the deaf and hearing worlds—even where there is a strong desire to overcome it—was made most concrete for us by an incident that happened to Ms. Walker. Her parents had driven her from their home in Indiana to Cambridge, Mass., where she was to begin at Harvard. After dinner they said their goodbyes in the restaurant. Her parents went to their motel and Ms. Walker went to her dorm room. But because of the strange bed and the impending first-time separation from her parents, she could not sleep. In *The New York Times Magazine* of August 31, 1986, she tells how lost and lonely she felt:

> In the dark, I felt more forlorn than ever. I waited until I thought [my roommate] was asleep, got up, put my clothes back on and walked outside. I didn't know where I was going. I headed toward what looked to be the busiest street and discovered Massachusetts Avenue. Mom and Dad had told me that was where the Holiday Inn was situated. I wandered up and down the sidewalk and found myself in front of their hotel.
>
> I made my way to their room on the third floor and, as I raised my knuckles, it dawned on me that knocking would do no good. I knew they were awake; I could hear the television. I took a notebook paper out of my purse and bent down to shove it underneath the door, working it in and out. There was no response. I tried crumpling up a small piece of paper to throw into the room, but I couldn't get it between the jamb and the door. I pounded on the gray metal, thinking they might feel the vibration. I must have stood there for 20 minutes, hoping Dad might come out to get ice from down the hall or perhaps go to the car to retrieve a bag. But he didn't.

That impenetrable steel door is a metaphor for the looming barrier that stands between the world of the hearing and the world of the deaf—even where there is a desire to overcome it. But overcome it some people do. And one of the ways they do is through dance.

Gallaudet Dance Company

The country's leading organization for dancing by deaf people is Gallaudet University in the nation's capital. But even there, the idea that deaf people could and should dance is comparatively recent, beginning only in 1955. Why was dance so late in coming to a 123-year-old institution which exists solely to educate deaf people? The answer: it simply had never occurred to anyone—even at Gallaudet—that deaf people could or should dance! In 1955, Dr. Peter Wisher, a professor of Physical Education, attended a ceremony in the chapel of the college and for the first time saw a student reciting *The Lord's Prayer* in American Sign Language. The graceful beauty of the signs impressed him, but more important, they caused him to ask out loud why deaf people were not dancing, using the ASL signs as foundations for the dance movements.

Professor Wisher's question rolled like a thunderclap across the Gallaudet campus and soon a dance club was formed, the members meeting a couple of times a week for an hour of fun and socializing. Soon the group was being asked to perform at functions both on and off campus. And before much longer, *The Gallaudet Dancers* was born, midwifed and directed by Professor Wisher. The group now consists of 15 dancers, give or take one or two as graduation thins the ranks and the arrival of new students builds them again. The students all are majors in other subjects and take dance as an elective. Their deafness ranges from moderate to total. The company has become famous and is invited to perform all over the country and overseas.

When Professor Wisher retired in 1981, he was succeeded by 39-year-old Dr. Diane Hottendorf, who has a Ph.D. in dance from University of Southern California. A tall, striking woman with a performer's presence, Dr. Hottendorf is hearing. For her post at Gallaudet she had to learn sign language. Included in her training, she told us, was a week of total silence in which she was permitted to use only sign language.

"About half the students who come to us for dance," she says, "were lucky and went to progressive schools

which gave them the benefit of dance training. The other half were unlucky in that their parents or their school clung to the old prejudice, 'Well, they're deaf; they can't hear the music, so what good would dance lessons do them'? That's the kind of hasty and faulty assumption the so-called 'normal' world is always making about people who have disabilities."

Diane Hottendorf, simultaneously finger-counting and rehearsing the Gallaudet Dance Company. From l. to r. Chris Smith, Sue Gill-Gould, Phyllis Beaton, Monika Valgemae and Valentino Vasquez. Gallaudet University

Many in the hearing audiences for whom Gallaudet Dancers perform have long-standing misconceptions about how the deaf manage to dance so well. Some believe the dancers use hearing aids to hear the music. Hearing aids are indeed a blessing to some deaf people, but to others they are a nuisance because the aids often distort sounds. Some hearing people believe the dancers feel the vibrations of the music through the floor. They don't: for one thing, they run and leap so much they are above the floor as often as they are on it; and concrete floors don't vibrate.

The secret held by deaf dancers is that the music is solely for the benefit of the hearing audience: those who are dancing don't need it. What enables them to dance is an exquisite sense of timing developed only after many, many hours of practice. So much practice is necessary because deaf dancers don't have the external cues provided by the music. When Gallaudet dancers begin to learn a new dance the first thing they do is put their hands on the enormous speakers in their studio to feel the beat. In that way they learn how fast their count should be for the piece. They don't work on the dance until they get the rhythm down pat. If the music has a heavy bass beat the dancers may be able to feel the beat in their breastbones. It is the *rhythm* they work to capture, *not* the music.

Dr. Hottendorf explains the difference between music and rhythm:

"Rhythm is internal. Being able to hear the music has nothing to do with being able to dance. Although music and dance are inseparable in the minds of most hearing people, they are two separate arts. Dance does not depend on music. Dance is an independent art and can be performed alone. My dancers count the time, the same as musicians do. We work very hard at getting and keeping the tempo."

34

But since the rhythm is internal, in the course of a performance the dancers often develop slight variations in their timing. There are always some dancers, however, who can hear some of the notes, either the high or the low, depending on the nature of their hearing impairment, and watching them helps the totally deaf dancer who is straying from the rhythm to get back on cue. They also watch each other more closely than hearing dancers do. They give each other visual cues about the rhythm, and dancers in the wings often show the count with their fingers to help out those on stage.

"Now I don't think deaf people have a better or worse sense of rhythm than anybody else," cautions Dr. Hottendorf. "Some deaf people have a wonderful sense of rhythm, but some don't, just like the rest of the people in the world. But an advantage they do have is that they *see* better. Not that they have better than 20/20 vision, but they really *look*. Most hearing people are aware that blind people develop very sensitive hearing, because they have to depend so much on sound to interpret the world around them. In much the same way, because deaf people have to depend so heavily on their eyes for their information about the world, they develop more sensitive sight. Their eyes notice very slight gradations of light that most hearing people wouldn't, and they see delicate movements more easily and clearly than most hearing people would.

"I once taught finger spelling to a hearing photographer and she picked up all the minute differences between the movements very quickly. A short time later I taught finger spelling to a couple of models who were curious about it. But with them I had to really work at it and repeatedly show them. When I thought about the difference, I realized that the photographer could *see*, and that's what made her a photographer.

And that probably is what makes someone a painter, too: they have bothered to take the time to learn to really observe. The eyes of deaf people aren't any different, but they know how to capture the visual moment, to really observe. Visually speaking, deaf people are generally more perceptive than the rest of us. Their lack of hearing makes them visual learners, so dance is one of the easiest things to teach them. Their language is movement."

When a hearing audience is brought face-to-face for the first time with the fact that deaf dancers don't need the music, the effect can be electrifying. During a performance in the Bahamas in the summer of 1983, the music tape broke. The dancers, of course, did not know this and kept right on dancing. The audience loved it and gave them a standing ovation.

The Company gives a couple of overseas performances each year and about 40 performances in the U.S. Director Hottendorf says the Gallaudet Dance Company has two reasons for being:

"The first is to provide dance opportunities just for the sake of dance; to provide our students with the joy of dancing and performing. Our aim is the same as that of all the rest of the activities that Gallaudet provides: to produce a well-rounded person. Many of the students in our dance classes came to Gallaudet thinking that dance was something they couldn't do and being able to do it gives them confidence. At a social function, a wedding or a party, because they can dance they are not outsiders, they are part of the group, they mix in easily: on the social level, a little bit of ability or knowledge can go a long way. And for those who are at a higher level of dance—the members of the dance company—I think they gain even more confidence, more self-esteem. Being able to dance well allows for them to enter the area of leadership.

"That alone is enough reason for the Company to exist. But our second mission is equally important. We feel that when the deaf world presents dance to the hearing world a lot of psychological barriers drop. We have a significant impact on our hearing audiences because we hit hard at assumptions the hearing world makes about being deaf and the hearing world begins to realize these assumptions are faulty. They learn that deaf people are able; that they can dance and maybe do a lot of other things that hearing people hadn't really believed the deaf could do. There's no doubt that our performances promote greater acceptance of the deaf world by the hearing world.

"I believe there is no one who is not disabled in some way. We all have our strengths, yes, but we all have our weaknesses, too. For example, I know a lot of so-called 'normal' people who can't follow time. What basis do they have for judging whether deaf people can learn to dance well? A lot more people in the hearing world need to understand that *all* of us have weaknesses—disabilities they are, really—and come to accept others for whatever they are.

"What a terrible term 'normal' really is! 'Normality' for you is simply what you are accustomed to. Now for me, a normal class is a class of deaf students. But I also have deaf/blind students. This year I have a nice young man, Stephen Ogilvie, in my ballroom class and he is deaf/blind. So he brings something extra, something different—his blindness—into my 'normal' deaf class. He performed on stage during our Spring concert, alone, without an interpreter and he did wonderfully well. He did a very good job with the Charleston. I also taught him the Cha-Cha and the hard thing in that is the turn, a full turn followed by a half turn. I taught him by moving him, dancing with him, and the interpreter relayed my instructions through touch. Stephen is bright and he learned it quickly. Teaching him is a joy. When I accomplish something with him I feel as much joy as he does."

Another accomplishment of Dr. Hottendorf is the establishment of Dance as a university minor subject.

"Through the Dance Minor," Dr. Hottendorf says, "students have the opportunity to choreograph; to work with sign language; to develop skills in ballet, jazz, tap and modern dance. They can start on the road to becoming dancers, choreographers, or dance therapists."

A member of the Dance Company is Lonnelle Crosby, 20, a first-year student. A major in Communication Arts, he has been hard of hearing since birth. Lonnelle had previous dance experience with a group of four men who danced in nightclubs in Lonnelle's home town of Joliet, Ill. When asked if dancing had done anything for him, a broad smile lit his face:

"Boy, it's done a lot," he exults, speaking and signing simultaneously. "It makes me think positive and I feel wiser about myself. When I first got here and watched the dancers in the Company I told myself I couldn't ever do that. Now when I get on the *barre* I find it shocking because I can do it. I'm studying jazz and ballet and tap and I'm getting to like each field better. The more I learn, the more graceful I get and that makes me want to learn more. My major is Communications and I believe dancing is very much a part of communications. When I graduate I would like to get a job as a dance instructor."

Another first-year student in the Company is Sherry Rome, who lives in a suburb of New Orleans. While she was in high school she tried out for the dance group but didn't make it. When we interviewed Sherry, Dr. Hottendorf told us she rated her, along with Lonnelle, as two of her top three dancers. Sherry is completely

38

deaf. Asked why she dances, she replied, with Lonnelle interpreting her signing into speech:

"I do it to relax and to keep in shape. I don't want to be a professional. I like it because we have fun as a group. We help each other a lot, like with counting the time. We help each other with our studies, too. If you have a problem in a course, someone in the group who is good in that area will help you. You can ask them and they'll help you. We're like brothers and sisters that way. I still get nervous when I perform, both before and during the performance."

The talk turned to parents and their reaction to the dancing of their children.

"My mom was surprised when I told her that Gallaudet had a dance group," said Lonnelle. "She didn't think deaf people could dance. I told her that I had been accepted for the Dance Company and when I went home for vacation she asked me to show her what we did. She was so amazed that what she did was take me right away to all her friends and some of our relatives and made me show them what I could do."

Sherry had a similar experience:

"Before I came to Gallaudet I couldn't do any kind of physical activity. I wanted to stay here during the summer to dance and my mother didn't want me to. She said it would be a waste of time because I could never learn to dance. But then a couple of TV networks did stories about the Gallaudet Dancers, with me in them and I told my Mom to watch. She was shocked: shocked! She had never seen me dance. And when I got home that summer she made me show her what I could do and then she piled me in the car and drove me to see every other member of the family and I had to show them all."

The third top dancer named by Director Hottendorf is Lily Chin. She was born to Chinese parents in Trinidad in the British West Indies but grew up in Toronto, Canada. When we talked with her in the summer of 1987, the 24-year-old Lily was a senior majoring in Home Economics and had been a member of the Dance Company for more than four years. Like Sherry, she does not want a career in dancing. What then, she was asked, keeps her interested in dancing?

"When I first came to Gallaudet I was stiff and awkward, not very nice to look at. Dancing has made me flexible and graceful. I dance to enjoy myself, to get exercise and keep in shape. School work and exercise must be kept in balance; your body needs the balance. School work, studying, means pressure, particularly at exam time and when I come to the studio I can forget about school and concentrate on dancing. Dancing is a great escape for me."

Helping Dr. Hottendorf teach dance classes and with the endless artistic and administrative details involved in running the Gallaudet Dancers is Sue Gill-Gould, the company's assistant director. She grew up in Trenton, New Jersey. Her parents are hearing and she has two brothers, one hearing and one deaf. She did her undergraduate work at Gallaudet and went on to a Master's in Physical Education and Education of the Deaf.

Ms. Gill-Gould is 27, beautiful, vivacious and a terrific dancer. Many have told her she could make it as a professional dancer in the hearing world, but she prefers to keep on doing what she is doing. Ms. Gill-Gould is hard of hearing; without a hearing aid she cannot hear a normal conversation but can hear a loud telephone bell if it is in the same room. If someone in the same room shouts or speaks close to her ear, she can faintly hear the words. With the two hearing aids she normally wears, she can hear in muffled tones the words of a person speaking about three feet from her. Dr. Hottendorf says she brought Ms. Gill-Gould into the company in 1983 since she felt it was important to have a deaf leader because so few deaf young people are exposed to people like themselves who can dance and who have been given responsibility. "Sue functions for us as a bridge between the deaf world and the hearing world," explained Dr. Hottendorf.

Throughout her years in school, Ms. Gill-Gould went to dancing classes and did so well that she determined to make dancing her career. "When I was small I was terribly shy," she recalls. "Dancing pulled me out." Because she had some hearing, could read lips and could speak normally, her parents sent her to public school. But she missed so much of what was said in the classroom that she was able to keep up and to be graduated only because her mother spent hours every night helping her with her lessons. Though dancing enabled her to overcome her shyness and become a member of her high school swim team and a basketball cheerleader, it did not overcome her diffidence about admitting to the world that she was nearly deaf. Throughout her years in grade school and high school she was able to hide her deafness completely from her teachers and from fellow pupils, even some good friends. But her attitude about her deafness changed when she stepped onto the Gallaudet campus. "For the first time in my life," she remembers, "I saw girls walking around with their hair pulled back and their hearing aids showing. I learned very suddenly that I didn't have to hide my deafness any more. I got so mad at myself for all those years when I'd worn my hair over my ears to hide my hearing aids."

After succeeding in the educational mainstream alongside hearing students for so many years, Ms. Gill-Gould says she decided to go to a university for the deaf because of the Dance Company—"and to meet people like myself."

Dr. Hottendorf and Ms. Gill-Gould have joined together and founded the National Dance Academy of the Deaf. They hold classes in dancing and tumbling for children aged 4 to 12, both deaf and hearing. The classes in Washington are a pilot for similar classes they hope to establish around the country. The teachers for these classes would be brought to Gallaudet for training. The two, along with Gina Oliver, Director of Campus Recreation, also have made a nonprofit videotape on aerobics titled *Sign and Sweat* with instruction in signing, voice and captions.

When asked if she intended to stay at Gallaudet, Ms. Gill-Gould shook her head vigorously in assent:

"Dancing with the Company gives me great joy. I have joy when I communicate with the audience. Seeing them smiling while I am dancing gives me joy. And I also very much enjoy sharing my knowledge with the students, teaching them new stuff, watching them grow. I love what I do and it makes me basically a happy person. The students respond well to me. They like the idea that I'm quite hard of hearing like them. I like being a role model for them. I'm glad I'm here and able to be that."

Dancer
Gwen Verdon

Among the hearing, the extraordinary life history of one of the world's great dancers is irrefutable testimony to the power of dance as a therapeutic medium. Younger readers may not recognize her name, but their parents will. In the fifties and sixties, Gwen Verdon was Broadway's dancing superstar, appearing in

Sue Gill-Gould who came to Gallaudet because of the Dance Company. She is now the Company's Assistant Director. Gallaudet University

a string of musical hits which included Cole Porter's *Can Can* and *Damn Yankees*, which ran for more than 1000 performances. The red-haired pixie who stood all of five feet, four-and-a-half inches, high-kicked the theater critics into such pirouettes of praise as "Verdon is a kaleidoscopic combination of Chaplin, Garbo, and a Picasso harlequin."

But Ms. Verdon's feet weren't always so nimble. She recalled for us:

"I was born disabled. My spine curved very badly and I couldn't hold my head up straight. My legs were badly bent and I was knock-kneed. My legs were so twisted that I had to wear corrective boots and braces. The doctors predicted that I would never be able to walk without crutches or a cane. They wanted my mother to let them try to straighten my legs by breaking them and then resetting the bones.

"But my mother was a dancer, a professional dancer, and she told the doctors 'no.' She knew how strong a dancer's leg muscles get and she figured if my leg muscles got strong they would act like splints and force my bones to go straight. So beginning when I was about two she started teaching me to dance and worked hard on my coordination."

The therapy worked so well that at the age of six Gwen was billed at the Loew's State Theatre in Los Angeles as "the world's fastest tapper."

Ms. Verdon has returned her mother's favor many times over. Throughout her career she has taught dance, coordination and movement to injured athletes and other disabled adults and children. She explained to us that teaching the disabled to dance is no different from teaching anyone else:

"I work with them the same way I would work with any dancer who is just beginning. Disabled people begin just as any dancer begins, so it's no different at

44

all. All that dancing really is is communication. If you feel something, then you are dancing. You don't need words. The minute they express emotion with their bodies they are really dancing. When they learn to allow themselves to feel, I can turn them into dancers. And the movements don't have to be pantomime like what Marcel Marceau does. The basis of all movement, of all acting, is the inner mind and it trains their eye for dancing and their movements. They start absorbing things. Dancing is really an attitude, just an attitude.

"If you can think about dance, about movement—if you can even *think* about it—you can do it. With some disabled people there may be some limitation, of course. But even the finest dancers in the world always develop their own special styles because that's the way they have to learn to dance to overcome a limitation of some sort. Some of these limitations, of course, may be more than what Fred Astaire had, but all dancers— all people—have some."

VSA's New Visions Dance Project

The day we talked with Ms. Verdon she was helping to teach a class of visually impaired students during the 1984 VSA Festival at the John F. Kennedy Center for the Performing Arts in Washington, D.C. The class was part of VSA's New Visions Dance Project, a program of instruction in modern dance for the disabled. In 1981, Wendy Amos, an instructor with the Alvin Ailey Dance Theatre in New York City, was teaching a course in the Pilates method of exercise, which is much favored by professional dancers. The exercises are done slowly but with great precision and an exact sequence of movements. The teacher's instructions must be lengthy, accurate, clear and precise. A blind

45

woman joined the class and found that because of the clarity of the instructions she could perform the exercises correctly and well, about as well as the non-disabled students. She suggested to Alvin Ailey that the class would be beneficial to other visually impaired people. The idea she planted with Mr. Ailey flowered in less than a year into the New Visions Dance Project.

The program began in 1982 as a cooperative venture between VSA and the Alvin Ailey Dance Theatre. The first group was limited to blind teenagers, students from a couple of New York City schools. The concept was quickly broadened, however, to include people with a wide range of disabilities and of any age. There are similar programs now in more than a dozen cities with students ranging in age from seven to 74. Lesson plans and an audiocassette are available for any teacher, school or organization that wants to begin a program.

"The disabled have just as important a part to play in the arts as the rest of us," Mr. Ailey explains. "We believe the arts are for everybody, not just the elite few. Our goal is to give blind people an opportunity to free themselves, a means to explore space, the air, to get a feeling of self-worth, of their place in the world, to conquer the instrument of their own body. When they feel they can create something with their own body they feel more a part of life. And that does a lot for their self-esteem."

A typical dance program consists of a 90-minute session once a week. The classes usually start with stretching exercises and often include African and Caribbean rhythms and movements as well as practice in balance and coordination techniques. The students also may be familiarized with a variety of musical instruments. One student in the New York program was Fay Reisner, who is in her seventies and is legally blind:

"It doesn't matter how old you are," she said as she took a break during a session a couple of years ago, resting on the floor, with sweat dripping from her face and arms. "I feel like I'm 21." It was obvious to an observer that the spinal operation and four-way bypass surgery she had undergone had hardly slowed her. "I was tired of the senior citizens groups just sitting around. Coming here they make you feel like everyone else. Nobody is better than you are. They encourage you to try. I'm always the first one here and the last one home. I feel very proud of myself."

Alvin Ailey Dance Theatre
Wendy Amos

After the break the dozen student dancers, clad in black tights and with bare feet, swirled around the studio to a bongo beat. Since most of the students were blind or nearly blind, several instructor's assistants stepped in now and again to prevent incipient crashes. The instructor, Wendy Amos, ran the class through a series of mood movements. The students jumped, hopped, stalked, whirled and rolled on the floor to depict moods like "angry," "tired," "lazy," and "upset."

Ms. Amos is the Alvin Ailey dance teacher who developed the basis for the curriculum. An alumnus of the Dance Theater of Harlem, she was named VSA's Outstanding Educator for 1986. She recalled what happened with the students in her earliest classes in 1982:

"These were very shy students. They didn't want to wear leotards and tights. The boys were absolutely upset about wearing something so close-fitting, ex-

47

posing their bodies. In a way, I guess, they were feeling, 'Here I am, almost naked in front of the world.'

"For all of them, the dance program is not simply a creative experience. It is that, but it is also much more. It makes them more independent in their day-to-day living. It makes them feel good about themselves. It is a tremendous challenge to them. Many who had not been exposed to the arts gain not only an appreciation of dance, but they start going to concerts, begin to learn an instrument, go to museums. Many who did not travel independently before have learned to travel with confidence and with more grace and comfort."

The name New Visions is the invention of Carol Penn. "Vision, of course refers to the physical ability to see," she explains, "but it also refers to the ability—and the need—to be able to envision a better world in the future. I firmly believe everybody—*everybody*—deserves an opportunity to be a participating member of the community. I hope that one day the myths about the disabled and the prejudices against them—not only against them, but against everybody—will be dissipated. That's the goal I'm hoping to help achieve with my work—a vision of a new world that includes all of us."

Ms. Penn, 30, is now the national trainer for New Visions. In addition to being a dance teacher, she is also a Special Education teacher. Formerly with the Alvin Ailey organization, she now lives in Washington, D.C. She travels around the country to give training workshops for people who want to start dance programs for the disabled. At the invitation of the Chinese government she was part of a VSA team that gave a workshop in China in 1987 for teachers of the disabled.

In the U.S., in addition to opening up to bring in

students with different disabilities, the New Visions Dance Project also has opened up to professionals. Ms. Penn explains:

"It's not only professional dancers who are starting classes now, but physical education people, special education teachers, rehabilitation specialists and regular classroom teachers who teach the disabled.

"I've worked to develop concepts and language that will allow teachers who have no background in dance to be able to design sessions of creative movement for disabled students. My philosophy is that if you are working with a disabled person and you are able-bodied, healthy and can stand up straight—if you learn to look at that as creative movement you have something right there to teach your student. Many disabled students can't sit up straight, can't hold their heads up straight or can't walk straight and if you can help them to do any of those things you will give them a whole world of movement that before was closed to them.

"Most people who have no background in dance think of dance as performance on the level of *Swan Lake* and say they can't do that; but that's not the goal of this work. Our goal is to use movement as the key that will enable a disabled person to find a bridge to self-esteem, a sense of fulfillment, a sense of enjoyment. If a person can learn to sit up straight and hold his head up straight, then the world sees that person differently and reacts to that person differently. When you see a person who holds his head to one side or who is slumped over your response might be pity or a feeling that the person has no authority and you might ignore them. So I tell the teachers I am training to keep exploring within themselves, to think about the movements they take for granted but which the disabled students don't have access to. And I tell them that they have something valuable right there to give their students.

"I told the same thing to the Chinese teachers I was training in Beijing. Their exercise system called *T'ai Chi*, with its slow movements, is practically tailor-made for the disabled, but it just hadn't occurred to them to apply it. I told them not to copy from us Westerners, but to look around them and use their own forms, what they already had right there. Their reaction was wonderful: I could just see the light bulbs clicking on in their heads."

Ms. Penn worked with Wendy Amos, teaching the first sessions of the New Visions Project when the classes were limited to completely blind children:

"The students came from special schools for the blind, with teachers specially trained to work with the blind. And from that quiet, protective environment they came into our noisy, bustling studios where they had to mix in with professional dancers, regular students, young adults, old people, all different kinds of people. They had to learn to stick out their hands and say 'Hello, my name is Mary So-and-So.' So it was not only the dance experience in which they got to be creative, but it was the socializing experience. It was wonderful to see those children coming out of their shells and starting to blossom and to be not afraid to greet the world. The dance experience, particularly their experiences in performing for audiences, gave them that dividend.

"Dance is a discipline as well as an art form and that discipline translates into your daily life. If you can get yourself together to be in a pair of clean leotards and tights, to be presentable in the dance class, and go through many monotonous and often very tiring exercises, then somehow, the way our minds work, that translates into 'I get up in the morning; I pull myself together; I meet my responsibilities and life goes on.'"

What Ms. Penn had to say about the impact dance has on disabled students was perhaps best summed up by blind 12-year-old Michael Todd, who attended the VSA dance program at the County College of Morris in New Jersey. Declared Michael in a statement elegant in its simplicity: "Dance makes you feel good."

Washington's New Visions Dance Theatre
Carol Penn

In the summer of 1985 Ms. Penn founded and now directs the New Visions Dance Theatre in the District of Columbia, in which she works with visually impaired children. In 1986 the group gave 21 performances before an estimated 15,000 people.

"I have ten students in my dance group. One of them is Erik, who is 17. He has tunnel vision, has very little peripheral vision, can't see anything below his knees and not too much above the top of his head. When the school people sent him to me his visual impairment was affecting him profoundly. He was turned inward on himself and was severely depresseed. He had no friends and was extremely shy. If a stranger said 'hello' to him he would burst into tears. But now, two years later, he goes with me sometimes when I give teacher training workshops in and around Washington and he can teach the exercises and can lead the other dancers. He's even comfortable in an interview situation.

"Teaching dance to visually impaired students is a long process that is based on precise orientation of the body," Ms. Penn says. "We mainly do improvisation and we create movements around a theme. We are not trying to create dancers. We are trying to do something that contributes to their becoming fully functioning human beings who can enjoy what our society has to offer. I see the children grow from being shy and inward into expressive persons who are ready and able to participate, to meet new people and new situations."

A natural question about blind dancers, particularly young ones, who are performing on a strange new stage is: are they not in danger of falling off and injuring themselves? Ms. Penn laughed:

"Blind and nearly blind people are very good at memorizing kinesthetic patterns in space because their lives literally depend on that ability. They know there are ten steps to the coffee table. When we are to perform on a new stage we arrive two to three hours ahead of time and we walk the stage so that they know that from the back wall to the front edge there are 30, 40, 50 or however many paces. And after that they rely on their kinesthetic memory. For sighted dancers moving well in space means trying to put over an aesthetic ideal; for my children it's a survival skill and they're very good at it."

Possessed of an elegantly slender dancer's body, Ms. Penn has a warm personality that makes it easy for people to learn from her. Nonetheless, it must take some doing to get a blind child to understand and then correctly assume say the five positions of ballet or simply a *port de bras* or a *plié*. How is it accomplished?

"That's where you find the greatest difference in teaching the visually impaired. I use a lot of patterning. Take a *plié*, for instance, to pattern it I touch the heels of my hands and fingertips together and form my hands into a diamond shape and have my students feel the pattern. Then I explain exactly where their toes and heels should be and where their knees should be. Likewise, for a *port de bras* I'll have them pattern the picking of a flower. Patterning generally works fine, but if a student doesn't get the pattern, I'll place their arms in the correct position."

Asked how she came to be involved in work with the disabled, she explained:

"I spent three years with the Alvin Ailey organization and at the end of that time I knew that while I wanted to be nothing else but a dancer, dancing by itself just wasn't enough. I felt incomplete. I needed something to dance *about*. I wanted to be able to say so many more things to people. I wanted two things: to expand my own dancing and to work with people I felt were disfranchised from the creative arts experience. I knew that would give me something to dance about. You see, I really grew up with that feeling. My father would talk about social responsibility, but my mother would take me with her into wards of the psychiatric hospital where she was a nurse and I got to interact with the patients. From the time I was a little kid I felt it was not fair that these institutionalized people, especially the children, couldn't have fun."

Break Dancer
Eddie Fernandez

The power of dance—even Break Dancing—to change lives can also be seen in the case of Eddie Fernandez. He is a 17-year-old Hispanic resident of Baldwin Park, California, and appears on the cover of this book. As a result of polio when he was an infant, Eddie needs leg braces and elbow crutches. But he does a spectacular—even by nondisabled standards—break dance, a demanding form of dance which originated on ghetto streets. During it he turns his crutches to advantage by flinging himself into the air upon them and doing an upside-down walk. And in the best approved Break

Dance fashion, he has learned to spin rapidly while standing on his head.

With about five years experience as a dancer, Eddie is good enough to be paid for performances. He has performed in Arizona, in Washington, D.C. and in Mexico, among other places. Through his dancing he has met Nancy Reagan and Sylvester Stallone. The money he has earned is in a trust fund, and when he finishes high school in 1988 he will use it to study to be a fashion photographer. Asked what he thinks is the best thing dancing has done for him, Eddie responds:

"It gets me a lot of respect."

CHAPTER THREE

Dance II
Arabesques and
Wheelies

*You can't tell someone wheelchair dance
is impossible for them.
If you do, you will kill the dream
and the whole organism will shrink.*

—BOB ALEXANDER

Some who have not seen an example of it might regard the term *wheelchair dance* as an oxymoron like *an optimistic pessimist* or *brilliantly stupid*. Wheelchair dance has nothing in common with wheelchair *square-dancing*, which is really a social occasion set to music and for many a valuable pursuit in its own right, but quite different in concept and execution from wheelchair dance.

Dance Teacher
Anne Riordan

A pioneer in wheelchair dance who also is the country's leading teacher of this art form is a woman whose life in dance has been as extraordinary as Gwen Verdon's in the overcoming of major physical problems. She is Anne Riordan of Salt Lake City. A ballet dancer, she was stricken with rheumatoid arthritis when she was in her mid-twenties. When increasing pain forced her to stop dancing professionally she was devastated and believed her life was over. Eventually she shook off her depression and decided she "had to retool my life." Retooling meant returning to the University of Utah, where she had majored in dance in what is one of the best dance departments in the nation, to work for a graduate degree in Special Education. Why Special Ed? Ms. Riordan, now 53, recalls:

"I hadn't any idea what Special Education was. At that time the disabled weren't visible. They were kept in back bedrooms or in institutions. I really hardly even knew what a disabled person was. But I felt I could teach and I needed to do something to earn a living. I really stumbled into the field because of my own needs. So my being in Special Education is really an accident."

It was one of the happiest accidents ever to occur at the intersection of dance and disability. After taking her degree, Ms. Riordan began teaching teaching mentally handicapped students. Ms. Riordan remembers:

"Though my disability, my arthritis, prevented me from dancing publicly on a stage, there was still a dancer inside me. I still *wanted* to dance, *needed* to dance, and also, because of the arthritis, I needed to move. So behind the closed doors of my classroom, with only the kids as my audience, I sometimes danced. At first it wasn't altruistic, I wasn't doing it for them, I was doing it for my own needs. But the kids were fascinated and excited by what I was doing. That was the beginning and since then we've never looked back."

The beginning was all experiment. Ms. Riordan gradually introduced her retarded pupils to structured body movement. They were so enthusiastic that before long they were putting on lunch-time dance performances, thereby launching their teacher on a new career, which began in 1972 when the Work Activity

Center for Handicapped Adults in Salt Lake City asked her to develop a similar dance program for mentally retarded adults.

As she had experimented with dance for her grade-school pupils, it was not long before Ms. Riordan was experimenting with the adults at the Work Activity Center. She introduced improvisational dancing, beginning by directing the attention of her students to their bodies, getting them to explore how they bent and could twist, how their arms and legs could move in the same direction or in opposite directions. When they understood these fundamentals, Ms. Riordan showed them how bodies can move through space and how they relate to other bodies moving through space at the same time. Thus was born the Sunrise Dancers. At first their audiences were parents, but soon the group began to get invitations to appear outside their home base of Salt Lake City. They have performed in California, Ohio, Arizona and Mexico.

After each performance Ms. Riordan speaks to the audience. What she tells them is this:

"It's important for the disabled to have fellowship with persons like themselves, but it is just as important that they have fellowship with persons unlike themselves. In bringing unlike areas of society together—the 'normal' and the 'disabled'—both benefit equally: emotionally, creatively, socially and spiritually."

These days a good deal of Ms. Riordan's time is spent teaching teachers of the disabled the special teaching techniques she has developed. She travels around the country, giving workshops at the rate of ten or a dozen a year. She is a full-time assistant professor of modern dance at the University of Utah.

The dancing of the Sunrise group was such a success, both from the point of view of the participants and their audiences, that Ms. Riordan branched out and formed Sunrise Wheels, a group of wheelchair dancers. Wheelchair dance is still pretty much out on the cutting edge of dancing concepts for the disabled and in this, as in so much of her work, Ms. Riordan has been a pioneer.

"With my first group of people in wheelchairs I hadn't a clue as to what I was going to do. But as I did before, I just experimented. I'd take them out of their wheelchairs and onto the floor. I had them help me choreograph dances they could do with the help of other people. We came up with some spectacular things."

One of those spectacular things was captured on videotape in 1981. Ms. Riordan danced with Mike Molesky, a man then in his late twenties who is in Sunrise Wheels. It was his first such dance encounter and as it begins the viewer sees his face is closed and distant, showing apprehension about what might come.

"I had a special warmth about Mike," recalls Ms. Riordan. "Our first encounter was hesitant. At the beginning I sensed a challenge from him. Not verbally, but a feeling of what's going to happen? How am I going to feel about me? I was certainly projecting my feelings about how he sensed me, and I realized we needed to have other kinds of communication with each other before we moved together. I said, 'We're going to dance together.' He replied, 'I'm not going to do any wheelchair square-dancing.' I told him that was not what I had in mind. What I did was to put myself in his hands. I told him he was a lot stronger than I was and he was going to manipulate me, take cues from me and we were going to have a conversation."

As the dance progresses, Mr. Molesky's tension visibly lessens and he begins to enjoy the exchange. Sensing this, Ms. Riordan moves into his chair with him.

Anne Riordan improvising in a "goodbye" dance, where at the end of the class everyone gets a chance to dance. L. to r. are Clair Durfee (in the chair), Duke DeForest and Richard Daly.

Ron Scott

She arranges herself in a graceful dancer's posture, legs drawn up with her feet resting on his knees, her hands above her head, and since she is partially turned toward him, one arm frames his head. It's a composition as spectacularly beautiful as it is unexpected. Her partner responds equally spectacularly, putting his chair into a sustained "wheelie," while—through what can only be an exquisite sense of balance—turning the chair through a rapid series of half-circles and simultaneous rocking movements without disturbing her pose. Later in the dance, he tips the chair all the way back and slides out of it on to the floor. He and Ms. Riordan then execute a series of graceful arm and upper-torso movements.

The dance, which lasts about ten minutes, is extraordinary in its sensitivity, for the communication apparent between the partners, and for the grace and beauty of their physical exchanges.

"It's been a challenge for me to be able to work with Mike," Ms. Riordan explains, "because we've been able to communicate on various levels. And to watch him get another sense of who he is and another dimension for himself was a thrill.

"As our dance progressed I felt Mike was showing his soul to me. I think it's difficult for a young man in a wheelchair to dare to show so much. I know he was struggling: I could see it in his eyes. Sometimes it's easier to show emotional states like that without words—because you don't have to justify them or defend them. They just exist!

"You know, for lots of people in wheelchairs, particularly those who have little mobility, most of the human contact they have is with people who take care of them, feeding them, toileting them and putting them to bed, and generally that is not the caring kind of human contact that we all crave. Wheelchair dance gives them that; it's very personal. It conveys a feeling of intimacy. I have found dance is is both an easy and a great way to communicate. When you dance together it is easier to get a connection with people because it's communication without words. You can get outside the prison of your own skin and connect with another human being. We all have the same needs. We all have the same joys and feeling and thoughts. And we all have the same need to create and express ourselves. I think that's one of the hardest ideas to embrace, that we're all coming from the same place: we just have different colorings."

Dancers
Bruce Curtis and Joanne Grady

Another who has found wheelchair dance to be liberating and exhilarating is Bruce Curtis of Berkeley, California. Mr. Curtis, 36, is a community organizer who has worked for the civil and human rights of the disabled in the U.S. and in Central America for more than a decade. He has used a wheelchair since a spinal-cord injury made him a quadriplegic 19 years ago. He began dancing in 1984 and his teacher and first partner was Joanne Grady, who is Director of the International Program for VSA.

"Bruce has been an inspiration for me," says Ms. Grady. "I arrived in Washington to go to work for VSA and Ralph Nappi, who was then co-director, introduced us. We hit it off right away and knowing I was a dancer and performer, after a while he asked if I could help him to dance. Although he is a quadriplegic, his arms have movement and flexibility."

"I had just turned 17 when I was injured," recalls Mr. Curtis, "and all the dancing I had ever done was the awkward shuffling around that passes for dancing among self-conscious teenage boys. So I never learned how to dance. Joanne and I had become good friends

61

and I knew of her dance background and that she had a generous heart so I got up enough courage one day to say to her that I would like to explore what it would be like to dance. I hadn't ever really danced and I didn't know what it meant, or how I could go about it but I would like to try and would she help me? She said she'd be happy to.

"We went to a small studio and put some music on. She didn't know what to do with me any more than I did. She first tried approaching it as she would when working with a class, like 'let's try these exercises.' But I told her that didn't feel good. So we just experimented around with what I could move and how I could move. I was looking for something that was flowing and approximated the cultural image that is ballet, but my understanding of what dance was about was just rudimentary. We explored, however, and gradually I started seeing some interesting movements occur that I'd never seen before. From that experience emerged an image in my mind of a choreographed piece that had a story behind it."

"So we choreographed a dance to Pachebel's *Canon in D*," says Ms. Grady. "We had a great time doing it. Bruce wanted to perform it publicly, but I said I wanted to videotape it so we could see what it looked like. We did it at Gallaudet and the tape came out beautifully. We both were amazed at what we had accomplished. The piece is six minutes long and the tape has been all over the U.S. and in many countries. We called the dance *Moonrise*, and there's a reason for the name."

During this time, Mr. Curtis went to Mexico to help in David Werner's Village Health Program. (Mr. Werner is a disabled artist whose extraordinary work is described in chapter nine.) Mr. Curtis' job was to show disabled villagers who couldn't afford wheelchairs how they could make them out of bicycle wheels and piping that was available and cheap in Mexico. They were trying to show the villagers how they could help themselves, what was possible for them. They also invited Ms. Grady to lend a hand.

"David and Bruce called a meeting," Ms. Grady recalls, "about this and we carried to it people who had rarely been out of their homes, who had been hidden away by their families. These people had no wheelchairs or prostheses and certainly had no inkling that it was possible for them to do anything for themselves. David and Bruce wanted to convince them that, all things considered, it was possible for them to live pretty good lives. And as part of that effort Bruce and I danced to show what disabled people could do."

"It was in the Sierra Madre mountains," Mr. Curtis remembers. "A little village beyond the end of the bus route, that you had to take a donkey or horse to get to. On one side of the village was a football field, right on the edge of a high plateau, overlooking a river gorge and a beautiful valley. It was evening, but not yet dark, and the stars were coming out and all around were the mountains; beauty all around.

"I put a cassette of the *Canon in D* on my tape recorder and Joanne and I danced. As we did so I gained a feeling of what it must have been like for people to dance under the sky and the stars to celebrate life and the earth and the sky and the moon. I began to connect with a sense of why it was that people worshipped in places like this at night. The happiness swelled up in me and I had an incredible experience. During our dance the moon rose and became just visible behind a mountain top. So we named our dance *Moonrise*."

"The people of the village had a great reaction to the dance, very positive," Mr. Curtis says, "And when I saw that, something clicked inside me. I suddenly realized that in all my work on behalf of civil rights

63

for disabled people, what it amounted to really was trying to change attitudes. How do you raise the consciousness of people toward the disabled, including the consciousness of the disabled themselves? What can you do? What *should* you do?

"Everybody who is concerned with that subject has always used media, trying to inform and educate with words, facts, figures. If they thought to use emotion at all, it was in a negative way—bringing out feelings of guilt and remorse in people. I was very dissatisfied with that. So when I saw the terrific reaction of the villagers to a wheelchair dance and learned that their attitudes toward us and toward themselves had changed, I was very keen to learn more about that— how effective the engendering of positive emotions could be in changing the attitudes of people about disability. I made up my mind to further explore all this."

Soon after returning to the U.S. from Mexico, Mr. Curtis moved from Washington, D.C. to Berkeley. He continues to experiment with dance, which has had further profound effects on him.

"When I first arrived in Berkeley," he remembers, "I didn't know who to contact, who to work with or where to go to continue. After all, wheelchair dance isn't very common. Then I discovered Sproul Plaza on the University campus. People go there on weekends with drums and other rhythm instruments to play. I dropped in one day and felt the power of the drumming: evocative, a strong communal experience. And I felt my body moving to the rhythm.

"After several visits, I realized I was moving my body to the rhythm of the beat and that essentially that's what dancing is all about. As minimal as my movements were, I saw they were just as valid as those of someone who danced all over the plaza to the same music. My movements were valid for me. The issue

64

wasn't whether we were doing the exact same movements, or even equivalent or comparable movements, but that we both were essentially *doing the same thing*: moving our bodies to the rhythm and what it evoked in us. Now I could accept my motions as being dance and being perfectly fine.

"I had developed an internal awareness of what felt right—and my body was beginning to make movements that no one had taught me. My body was finding these movements by itself. That was fascinating for me: that in my body I now had an ally; I didn't feel I was having to fight my body to get it to produce movement. My body was giving me new information and new experiences.

"As a result of all this, I began to trust myself more. I trusted that what I was doing was right. And soon another fascinating experience came on me. When I danced I was happy, having a good time. I was excited and smiling, full of joy. And when another dancer—not disabled—looked into my eyes and I looked back, they would light up, smile, too, and be transformed. You know how people in groups are sort of self-contained and formal, with not a lot of exchange going on. They may be in almost the same spot, but there's a distance between them. I now often saw this fear between people evaporate through the fact that I had no fear in my face and no fear in my heart and joy in my eyes and was smiling; this touched the other person.

"I now decided the next thing I should try was to go dancing in a nightclub or a discotheque. I knew that if I could dance as I had been doing in a public square in daylight with crowds around, I could dance anywhere. But a club or discotheque has a social environment quite different from a public square and there are some social constraints. The intent in those places is dancing and people want you to dance and would like to see that you know what you are doing and can dance appropriately alongside them. So for me to get up from wherever I am sitting and to go out in front of people and dance—where the point of the place is to dance—is a very fearful thing. It's fear of rejection. Do you have any right to be there, to participate like that? You fear that what you are doing is beyond what is acceptable and enjoyable for others, that your presence may be distasteful. These fears arise mostly from your concept of your physical image and how well people may or may not accept you. And I don't think I'll ever get rid of that fear. But I have learned to transform it into a determination not to need the approval of others when I dance in a nightclub or discotheque."

Mr. Curtis has been extending and deepening his dance experience with work in Contact Improvisation. In this dance form the dancers aim to maintain a constant flow of contacts, communications, between them which are both physical and emotional. As the name states, the steps and movements are improvised. He has been dancing with Alan Ptashek, a movement educator and performing artist in body movement awareness, who is on the faculty of New College of California in San Francisco.

Of a videotape of Mr. Curtis and Mr. Ptashek dancing together, Ms. Grady says:

"They have been developing the most innovative wheelchair dancing I have seen. His partner lifts Bruce out of his chair, carries him and flings him around and then Bruce is on the floor, moving every ounce of what he's got to move. He seems to be in great shape and his body has been developed, where otherwise it would have atrophied. Dance has had a major impact on his life in terms of making him feel more in touch with his humanity."

CHAPTER FOUR

Drama
The Mind's Eye

For jobs we need the three R's,
But I think of art as the fourth R
—the one that helps us know who we are.

        —BERNARD BRAGG

For people who have limitations, physical and otherwise, theatre frequently can achieve results that are fantastic—and the word is carefully chosen.

Listen to Bob Alexander, who 21 years ago founded a company called Living Stage, which is devoted to involving socially and economically disadvantaged and physically and mentally impaired people in drama:

Living Stage
Bob Alexander

"Some years ago we were doing a one-day improvisational workshop with a group of young blind people and a 14-year-old girl began working with one of our actors, Larry Samuels. He set a scene where they were at the beach—there were a half-dozen or so other groups doing improvisations in the same room—and he told the girl he was a painter. She replied that she loved painting. Larry asked if she would like to go to his studio to see his paintings. 'Oh, I'd love to!' she cried. So they hailed an imaginary cab and drove off, with the girl describing—remember that she's blind—

the streets they were riding through. From her description Larry could tell that they were in New York City, in Times Square. Suddenly she yelled, 'Stop the cab! Stop the cab!' Larry told the driver to stop and asked her why. 'Do you see those keys lying on the sidewalk?' she asked. Larry said he did and she told him he had to get out of the cab and get them. When Larry asked why, she replied, 'Because they are the keys to my heart.'"

Though her phrase was poetic Larry Samuels and Bob Alexander saw nothing remarkable in it. After all, it was the sort of improvisational exchange that they do with the disabled almost every day. Only later did they learn that this was the first time the girl had spoken in seven years.

"It was clear to us," explains Bob, "that she had been harboring a poet inside, but since she had been so ostracized because she was blind she wasn't going to risk further put-downs by revealing her poetic nature. So she kept quiet—totally quiet—until she met an artist who gained her confidence and made it clear to her prior to the improvisation that she was in an environment in which she could feel safe and could let her imagination roam. Functioning as a sensitive artist, Larry was able to make intimate contact with her that probably could not have been made in any other way. And when he began the improvisation she was able to respond as she would have liked, no doubt, for a number of years to respond to others."

Living Stage is a community outreach project of Arena Stage, the nationally known theatre-in-the-round in Washington, D.C. The company may work

Robert Alexander, Director of Living Stage, shares a joyful moment with a young student.

with a group for a single session or for periods up to two or three years. Typically, groups of children and young people attend weekly two-hour sessions for 20 weeks. The number and frequency of sessions depends on the needs of the group and the workload of the Company.

A key to understanding how Mr. Alexander and his actors accomplish what they do in their special kind of theatre is that they don't make theatre *for* the disabled, but *with* them; and therein lies a world of difference.

"Disabilities can interfere with communication, learning and behavior," says the Company Director. "We use the art of theatre to liberate and channel in a positive direction the skills, attitudes and emotions that have become obscured in the child's struggle to overcome the handicap. What this theatre of ours is all about is expressing feelings: You use your mind, your voice and your body to express your emotions. We work to get a creative bonfire going inside the person—and to me that means we are getting in touch with the most magnificent part of the human being."

Living Stage consists of six performing personnel titled Actors/Educators and an on-stage musical director, backed by 13 support personnel. Just what the members of the group are capable of can be seen in a second case cited by Mr. Alexander, that of Susan and actor Gregory Jones.

"A few years ago after we had done a couple of sessions with a group of youngsters, their teachers said they would bring in a ten-year-old named Susan. But they told us, 'She's just a vegetable; can't do anything. However, if we bring her in she might just get a little something out of it.' They brought her in and when the children were having lunch I was stunned to see a teacher put food in Susan's mouth and actually move the child's jaw as if she didn't know how to eat. If I

70

had never before seen a self-fulfilling prophecy, at that moment I was seeing one in action: if people treat you like a vegetable, you become a vegetable. I don't know what her condition was. It might have been severe cerebral palsy, but it doesn't matter.

"We took her out of her wheelchair and put her on the floor. She immediately began hopping around on all fours. We then did an improvisation about becoming a piece of clay and what happens to you. Some people turned themselves into bricks, some into toys, others into beautiful sculptures. The improvisations went on for about an hour and then the children were asked to write poems based on what they had been doing. Susan couldn't speak, so Gregg constructed lines for her and she signalled that she liked a line or disliked one, by smiling for yes—her face lit up as though a hundred angels had taken her hand. For no, she screwed up her face as though she had just sucked the world's bitterest lemon. When it came her turn, Gregg said he would read the poem Susan wrote and she would dance to it. As he reads, she dances—lying on the floor. To me she looked like a Balinese dancer, or like a dainty, graceful poised animal. She paused where the pauses in the reading were. And at the end she froze her movements, with an arm extended and a leg back, because she knew it was the end. Her teachers' jaws dropped to their chests.

"As with the blind girl, that whole accomplishment was possible for Susan because she was interacting with an artist, not a clinician. I'm not putting down clinicians, but artists often can reach deep inside a person and release the imaginative power that has been locked up all their lives. The clinicians had diagnosed and psychologized Susan. They had *looked* at her but didn't *see* her—the artistry and passion that was in her but which she couldn't communicate in the 'normal' way."

71

Reports of many observers have convinced the authors that the results obtained by Living Stage can be described only as tremendous: reticent children begin talking, withdrawn youngsters become socially open, physical therapists are amazed when children begin to move in ways they never have been able to in therapy sessions. Mr. Alexander explains this last easily and with a laugh: "The therapists try to get them to move through calisthenics, which are repetitious and mechanical and boring. We get the kids so involved in being creative that they begin to move disabled or weakened limbs without even being aware they're doing it. You see, in the moment of artistic creation, one is whole and sane regardless of one's pathology, neurosis, psychosis or physical condition."

Each performance of this improvisational theatre is unique because it never happened in quite the same way before and will never happen in just the same way again. But underlying the spontaneity is a highly structured form. Before a performance the company of actors picks a theme that is relevant to the lives of the young people who will participate. For those who are older, age about 15 to 21, the themes range over the matters they worry about: drugs, racism, freedom, family, the courage to dream, wishes, love, friendship, hope. For younger children the themes are friendship, parents, siblings, animals. Living Stage now has a repertoire of more than 40 performance pieces based on these themes.

The acting company begins a piece with a musical jam session during which they create songs on the theme. The song-making is supported by strong, rhythmic music produced by many percussion instruments and an electronic piano. The audience enters the theatre space during this musical beginning and they are given instruments and encouraged to get involved musically, physically and verbally. The actors urge those who have little or no verbal ability to invent a vocabulary of signs, gestures and symbols.

When the music reaches a crescendo, it leads into the performance, which consists of poems, songs and abstract physical movements that communicate the feelings of the theme. At a critical point in the play the company stops the action and calls on the audience to provide the conclusion. The actors ask for alternate endings based on wishes, hopes, fantasies and unique visions of the world.

"We improvise based on the feelings and concepts that come out of that audience at that moment," says Mr. Alexander. "We ask them to tell us what is going on in their heads at that second and not what they were thinking or experiencing yesterday, or what they think is going to happen later. The most important thing to you as a member of the audience is to have an emotional context, and then the theatre will be directly related to your needs and dreams. A number of alternate endings usually are performed to illustrate how each person's perception has its own logic, validity and importance."

The piece always ends with a song that encompasses the theme that was illustrated. The actors now introduce themselves and begin to engage the audience in the work of theatre. The young people begin to create characters that express themselves, using whatever movement, sound or other ability they have to express their creativity. This work gradually becomes more complex and involving until each actor and each audience member becomes a character in an imaginary environment and they interact with each other to create an event of dramatic theatre. "In improvisational theatre *you* create the situation, the character, the dialogue, everything," Mr. Alexander says. "Kids have no problem with this; after all, it's what they do all the time when they play."

A Living Stage performance thus is much more than mere entertainment. It is a dialogue between the actors and their audience—both as human beings and as artists. Audience members are not passive observers; they experience theatre from the inside. Becoming characters—singers, dancers, poets, musicians—they express their deepest hopes, dreams and fears in a creative burst. The immediacy of the involvement with the artistic process triggers a lasting awareness of the relevance that theatre has to one's own life. The main objective of the performance is to bring people to understand that theatre is about real people who have aspirations, terrors, frustrations, dreams and hopes like themselves and like everyone else in the audience.

"The performance also reveals to the audience why people do what they do with each other," Mr. Alexander notes. "Repeated exposure to these experiences brings to participants the discovery that everybody is an artist in his own right and that—just as much as food or sleep—every one of us needs the release of creative expression."

The word *therapy* is anathema to Mr. Alexander. He vehemently denies it is what Living Stage is practicing. "The process that we get the kids involved in is a healing one," he says. "And anything healing—that makes people feel better about themselves, feel stronger, make discoveries about themselves—is therapeutic. And all of those things happen to you when you function as an artist. While the *consequence* of what we do is therapeutic our *objective* never is to provide therapy. What I and Living Stage are all about is empowering people so as to enable them to fall in love with their own creativity."

Every Special Education teacher, and perhaps many

Associate Director Jennifer Nelson of Living Stage, with a student from Sharpe Health School. The child is the King of Worms and Snakes. Jennifer is the King's servant.   Kelly Jerome

parents too, reading this description of Living Stage probably has been thinking: this all sounds terrific, but is there any carry-over after the child leaves the program?

"We find there is quite a bit," Mr. Alexander maintains. "Not long ago a 16-year-old high school girl told me she was in Living Stage as part of a daycare center program when she was four. She remembered the characters and situations and the environment she had created 12 years before. Kids very seldom see adults do what kids do—enter their world of make-believe. But they see us do it and it affects them deeply and stays in their consciousness. There is a big carry-over because their experience with us validates them as human beings. When they leave Living Stage they know that their creative thinking is right, that their choices are right, that no matter what anyone in the future tells them, they know their thinking and feeling is not wrong. At the Sharpe Health School for disabled children here in Washington the principal says new teachers who have never seen one of our sessions tell her that they can distinguish children who have been in a Living Stage program by their ability to concentrate, their ability to initiate, their ability to play with each other, cooperate with each other."

The National Theatre of the Deaf
David Hays

When it was founded in 1967 The National Theatre of the Deaf was a bold, even reckless idea whose start was little noticed; at its first performance the audience was just six curious souls. By the end of the show they were six clapping, cheering, stomping fans. And that has been the story ever since. A bold, even reckless idea when it began, NTD has become one of the most resounding theatrical successes of our time.

The key to what NTD is all about lies in the smallest word in its title: OF, which carries a world of meaning. The major meaning is that NTD is not theatre FOR the deaf, a company of deaf people who use sign language to communicate with audiences of deaf people. NTD is a mainstream theatrical company that has done nothing less than invent a new theatrical form for its performances to mixed audiences of deaf and hearing people. Measured against any professional theatre organization in the country, NTD is not merely average, it's outstanding. The Company represented the U.S. at the 1984 Olympic Arts Festival; it has won two Tonys, an Oscar, an Emmy and a fistful of other awards; made TV specials for CBS, NBC and PBS and appeared on Broadway; it has played in every state and has toured overseas twice as many times as any other American theatre company, performing in 24 countries and being the first American theatre group invited to perform in China. NTD has toured Europe nine times, the Far East twice, the Near East twice, Australia and New Zealand twice, the Caribbean once and the United States 37 times in the 20 years since its founding. NTD is American's number one touring theatrical company—by far.

Director David Hays, who is hearing and one of the founders of NTD, describes himself as "the proud artistic director of one of the best theatre companies in the world." Much of the success of NTD is due to Hays' vision of the art form that signing could become. Before NTD existed, he saw sign language as, in his words, "sculpture in the air." He saw the signs deaf people made not as crude gesticulation but as fluid, graceful elements of an image-rich language that is, like English, by turns both delicate and powerful. He was able to see the theatrical possibilities of signing because he was a successful world-class theatrical designer. His studying days were spent at Harvard and at the Old Vic in London on a Fulbright scholarship. He has designed sets for more than 50 Broadway shows and for more than 30 ballets for the New York City Ballet. He has consulted and designed for numerous theatres being built in the U.S. and Australia. Hays has won many awards as a set and lighting designer, including a couple of Obies.

The first notion that the deaf might be able to perform for hearing audiences came from the government. Education for the deaf has long been financed by the federal government. The administration of programs for the deaf is in the Office of Education of the Department of Health and Human Services. In the early sixties, the success of the highly acclaimed play *The Miracle Worker,* about the education of deaf and blind Helen Keller caused some people in the Office of Education to wonder if a Broadway production featuring deaf actors might be possible. They saw such a production as a way to put some deaf people to work so they could become self-supporting and not need government support. The officials approached Anne Bancroft, star of the play, and Arthur Penn, the director. And the designer David Hays. The three went to Washington to discuss the idea. While there they attended a production of *Our Town* by the deaf students at Gallaudet college. Mr. Hays was electrified by the grace, beauty and power of signing, seeing for the first time with his designer's eye the imagery that is inherent in the English language. Because of the prior film and theatrical commitments of Ms. Bancroft and Mr. Penn, the Broadway production featuring deaf actors never got off the ground. Haunted by the play he had seen at Gallaudet Hays determined to go on alone to establish a theatre of the deaf which would not be an occupational therapy sort of thing, but a highly professional theatre in which well-established actors from the hearing world would train talented deaf actors in the best of modern stage techniques. And that's the way NTD has always worked. Among those who have worked with the Company are Colleen Dewhurst, Jason Robards, Chita Rivera, Arvin Brown, Peter Sellars and Sir Michael Redgrave. These outside professionals teach under the auspices of the Professional School for Deaf Theatre Personnel, which has trained hundreds of actors and is an adjunct of NTD.

After his Gallaudet experience, Mr. Hays went on

to help establish the Eugene O'Neill Theatre Center in Waterford, Connecticut, but he managed to find time to keep alive the interest of the officials in the Office of Education to the point where they eventually committed money to launch NTD. To this day the Company continues to receive support from the Office.

What accounts for much of the success of NTD is that the Company and David Hays have done nothing less than invent a new theatrical art form. Until NTD there had been nothing like it before. The actors use sign language, but it is sign language that has been magnified for the stage. The result is visual wizardry of dazzling beauty which, in addition to "sculpture in the air," has been described as "music for the eyes." The signs have been theatricalized, enlarged beyond real-life dimensions. This stage language created by NTD is to normal sign language as singing is to ordinary speech. The Company combines these magnified signs with words spoken by the hearing actors who as they play their parts use both words and signs. So the audience both hears the dialogue and sees the play's language as it dances and floats on the hands of all the actors, both hearing and deaf. The signs are not only on the hands of the actors, for sometimes their entire body becomes a word, a thought, an emotion. The result is that the audience receives a clearer, sharper *enlarged* understanding of the spoken words. This synthesis is a new dramatic form in which the speech of the hearing determined from the beginning that NTD would mount the deepest and most complex language plays and they have done so: works like *Gilgamesh*, *Woyzeck*, *Volpone*, and *The Iliad*.

Deaf people were enthralled by the rave reviews and clamorous applause for NTD's first productions. They reveled in the adulation the hearing public heaped on deaf actors. But, irony of ironies, the productions of

NTD are too literary as yet for most deaf people, who are puzzled by the plays. There are two reasons for this. They are the two means of communication: NTD signing and the spoken word.

Most deaf Americans use a language called Ameslan, the abbreviation for American Sign Language. Ameslan is not English. It is a true language in its own right with its own style and form, but void of English declension and conjugation. It has a grammar and sentence structure, but not as understood in the English language. It is a language that relies on visual concept and requires the same sort of interpreting into English as French or Japanese does. Nearly all deaf Americans know how to fingerspell. American fingerspelling consists of a single hand shape for each letter of the English alphabet. It is used almost exclusively for proper names and technical terms. It is possible, of course, by using a combination of sign and fingerspelling to sign, quite literally, the English language. One's proficiency in signing English, however, is dependent upon one's understanding of the English language and the breadth of one's English vocabulary. The English language is a second language for many deaf Americans whose skills in English are minimal. These are the people who find the NTD difficult to understand, since on stage the NTD uses far more sign English than Ameslan. It is curious, but the language barrier sometimes facing the NTD exists, not between the NTD and the hearing public, but between the NTD and the the deaf public. It exists because NTD is a theatre *of* the deaf, not *for* the deaf.

David Hays is well aware of this problem and he shared his thoughts on it with us:

"Well, to begin with, most deaf people just are not used to seeing sign language on the stage. You need to see sign language frontally and very clearly and we play theatres that have large aprons or are three-quarters in the round, where not every member of the audience can see the actors frontally all the time. When a deaf person is sitting far back in the audience, the hand of the actor may not reach the eye as the magnified voice will reach ears sitting in the back rows of the Hollywood Bowl. So for deaf people NTD performances require a kind of intimacy which we cannot always guarantee for them and they will miss some words. But deaf people think that hearing people hear every word, though we don't. In the theatre we supply quite a bit of dialogue ourselves from the context. In fact, we go to operas in other languages and don't expect to understand many of the words. But we know the general lines of the plot and we have a sense of what's going on. We're relaxed about the situation. But in the world of sign language people aren't relaxed about understanding when things on stage are out of context for them and it takes them a while to catch up. They think hearing people have a kind of magic that makes every word crystal clear. They have no idea how difficult Shakespearean stage English is for most hearing people. It's understandable that deaf people feel frustrated when they feel a bit left out and have to try to catch up. But as the years go by they improve. We work as hard as we can to improve things, but the problems are there and we just can't wish them away."

The Company now consists of ten deaf and two hearing actors. They are headquartered at the Hazel Stark Center in Chester, Connecticut.

If NTD is pushing the deaf community to improve and expand its understanding of theatre, language and a new form of signing, thereby improving their ability to communicate with the rest of humanity, so NTD can be seen to be pushing hearing people into a greater understanding of both the needs and the capabilities of deaf people. Director Hays believes that in the past decade there has been a burst of knowledge and understanding about the deaf, a great advance in captioning of film and television programs and a general reversal of negative attitudes held by hearing people about deaf people. He feels that despite the frustrations that continue to exist, the position of the deaf minority in the U.S. "has zoomed." And though he can't prove it in black and white, Mr. Hays attributes a good portion of the improvement to the work of The National Theatre of the Deaf.

Only a year after NTD burst on the scene it produced a lusty offspring, The Little Theatre of the Deaf. There are several companies in this program, each composed of four deaf and one hearing actor. Designed to present to children a more intimate theatre than that of the parent company, LTD units perform short stories, fables, fairy tales and poems, usually in schools, parks, museums and libraries. These groups, too, have done extensive touring in Australia, Scandinavia, England, India and the West Indies. The success of NTD has encouraged deaf people around the country to form amateur theatrical groups. Mr. Hays estimates there are about 30 of these.

NTD is a shining example of the social changes that can be wrought by an art well practiced. Because of NTD's success and influence, opportunities for the deaf have opened in television and films. The greatest success so far for a deaf person in films was Marlee Matlin's great performance in *Children of a Lesser God*, her first film role, for which she won an Academy Award. In the same role on Broadway, Phyllis Frelich, who trained at NTD won a Tony award. Through the higher visibility of deaf people on stage and on television, deaf children have deaf heroes and heroines to emulate, and because of the success of NTD in an enterprise as public and as glamorous as theatre the entire deaf community is considerably more visible and more highly thought of than was the case 20 years ago.

Actor
Bernard Bragg

One of the founders of NTD with David Hays was Bernard Bragg, the famed deaf actor and mime, who also has been a leader in gaining recognition for deaf actors and their abilities. He helped in the development of the form of magnified sign which NTD actors use. Born deaf to hearing parents, Mr. Bragg came by his love of drama through his father, an actor and director in a nonprofessional theatre company that performed exclusively for deaf audiences. He began acting and directing as a student at Gallaudet.

In the early fifties Mr. Bragg went to a performance of the famed French mime Marcel Marceau, mostly because he wanted to see how a hearing audience would react to a silent performer. At the end of the performance, Mr. Bragg was too moved to rise for the standing ovation. "I never dreamed it would be possible to have a hearing audience so captivated," he says. Mr. Bragg headed backstage with pencil and paper to communicate with Mr. Marceau. "I've been doing pantomime all my life," he wrote. "Where can I study the discipline?" The world-famous French mime invited the American to a tryout performance the next day. He liked what he saw and invited Mr. Bragg to work with him in Paris during the summer of 1956. Under Marceau's direction, "I learned the physical grace, the flow, the balance," Bragg says. "The most difficult part was the breathing, because I can't hear myself. Breathing has a lot to do with emotions and must be in absolute harmony with whatever you are doing."

Bragg then launched a highly successful career as a mime, an actor and director, touring the U.S. and Europe many times. He acquired many awards for his stage work and for his work to advance the cause of deaf people in and out of theatre. For the first ten years of NTD he was an actor and administrator with the Company, recruiting actors and helping to adapt plays to the Company's unique form of sign language. He appeared in nearly 2,000 performances.

Bragg is now a consultant and teacher at Gallaudet, a free-lance performer who does one-man shows and improvisational mime on themes suggested by the audience at Second City in Chicago, and a playwright. In his teaching, as in his performing, Bragg aims to expand the ways that people communicate. "I encourage people to stretch themselves," he says, "to interpret with their faces, hands and bodies." Throughout his career one of his long-range goals has been to help achieve "open-mindedness toward our culture, as well as open-eyedness to our visual communication." Through capturing the imaginations of audiences, both deaf and hearing, Bragg has moved the world a little closer to that goal.

Gallaudet University
Theatre Arts Department

In contrast to NTD, Gallaudet's drama department concentrates on theatre *for* the deaf. The first plays on campus were presented in 1890 by a students' drama club. The college began offering formal courses in the 1930's and in 1963 the Department of Drama was formed. Since 1969 students have been able to major in drama, with a choice of two areas of concentration: production/performance or developmental drama. In the production/performance area, the college sticks largely to producing plays originally written for a hearing audience which have been rewritten into sign language as well as some plays written specifically for deaf theatre. The Department does three plays a year, with a fourth for children, which usually attracts about 5,000 youngsters. In the winter of 1987/88, the

Bernard Bragg, the famed deaf actor and mime, is signing the word "world." Gallaudet University

Department is presenting a joint production with the University of Maryland of *Children of a Lesser God*. Maryland will provide actors for the four leading hearing roles and Gallaudet will provide actors for the three deaf roles. Like NTD, the productions at Gallaudet use a second, speaking cast in a variety of ways. Sometimes they are integrated onstage, sometimes they are behind the stage and sometimes they do only voice-overs, depending on the style of the production.

The majors in developmental drama concentrate on discovering how drama can help in the development of children. They study puppetry, role playing, storytelling, the use of masks, mime and improvisational theatre. They also investigate how drama can aid learning for children in educational, recreational, therapeutic and social settings.

Another college where deaf students can study theatre is the National Technical Institute for the Deaf in Rochester, New York. It was established in 1968 by the Rochester Institute of Technology, a college for the hearing. Like Gallaudet, NTID offers three productions a year, usually featuring deaf actors signing the leading roles, with hearing voicing the action onstage. The plays are aimed at deaf audiences.

Model Secondary School for the Deaf

Adults in the professional theatre generally believe that you can hardly ever be too young to begin to learn the ropes of serious drama. And that's the way it is at the Model Secondary School for the Deaf, a 400-student high school which is on the campus of Gallaudet University and like Gallaudet, is financed by the federal government. In line with that philosophy MSSD offers freshmen a course titled *Introduction to Play Production* in which students get a taste of all aspect of theatre: writing, directing, acting and business management—and have to produce their own shows, which are considerably more complex and sophisticated than what most of us think of when we hear the phrase "high-school play". The result of this philosophy is that MSSD has a very strong drama department, from which top students go on either to the Gallaudet drama department or to NTD. As proof that you can't begin theatre too early, MSSD drama instructor Tim McCarty noted that almost without exception every student who was succeeding in the department or who had succeeded in the past had taken this freshman course.

"And," says McCarty, "the course has side benefits. For a lot of kids who come here from different parts of the country the beginning is tough. For a lot of them it's their first time away from home. They likely felt isolated in their previous schools. Many don't know sign language. What *Introduction to Play Production* does for them is it allows them to work with others on their project and to be creative. Also it provides a non-threatening way to learn sign language. Being involved in a production, which they have to be that first semester, they begin to make friends and to fit in. When they first arrive, many of our kids are frustrated because they can't communicate well. But sharing, of course, requires communication and starts them on the right road. When they leave here, all of our kids are pretty good communicators.

"Another side benefit—well, it's really much more than a side benefit—is that students who go through our drama program end up being much better readers. The process they normally go through to develop a character forces them to read intensively for comprehension, what the character is really thinking and feeling. So their reading skills improve tremendously."

Mr. McCarty hastened to point out that his department is not geared exclusively to turning out actors, directors and playwrights. If students just want to learn about theatre so they can have it as an avocation in later life, that's just fine. But for those who want to make theatre a career, MSSD provides lots of raw meat.

The reputation of MSSD's drama department has spread far and wide. They were invited to England, which is behind the U.S. in the opportunities available to deaf people, to demonstrate their abilities. Thirty-five people toured for four weeks in the summer of 1985 with the school production of *Godspell*, which Tim McCarty produced and directed. They performed at such prestigious places as Oxford University and Sadler's Wells. But for the students, the highlight of their trip occurred when they took a turn at the old British custom of *busking*, dressing up to give a street performance after which the hat is passed among the gathered crowd. On Saturdays these street performers, who might be regarded as semi-pros, gather at London's famed Covent Garden to do their thing.

In the plaza in front of Covent Garden, in which is set the first scene of *My Fair Lady*, a crowd of about 100 was watching the performances when the MSSD group arrived. They set up their sound equipment and launched into a 40-minute showcase of songs from *Godspell*. By the end of the first number, Tim McCarty recalls, the crowd had grown to about 800 and they were clapping and cheering. Forty minutes is a long time for a street performance, but at the end the crowd was yelling for more. When they passed the hat they got 75 pounds and felt terrific because street performances are chancy things, nobody can tell how they will turn out. The kids used the money for a big blowout closing night at Sadler's Wells. Says McCarty, "Kids are funny. They were far more impressed and pleased with what they had accomplished on a London street than in any of the theatres we performed in." MSSD students also have performed at a leadership conference in Rochester, New York, and at an international mime festival in Canada.

"Our program has achieved excellence by any standard and has been so recognized," says McCarty so firmly as to leave no room for doubt. "Our next task is to find centers for advanced training for our students and then to get them jobs and then to have them hired on the basis of their ability. I don't want any of my students ever hired because they are deaf, or *not* hired because they are deaf. And I don't want them playing only characters who are deaf. I think they should have the opportunity to perform almost any character."

Theatre Data Bank

A centralized referral system for both human and technical resources in theatre for people who are disabled has been put together and is being maintained at Wright State University in Ohio by Professor William Rickert, who is Associate Dean of Liberal Arts. The system is on a computer and consists of an annotated and cross-indexed listing of people who are working anywhere in the nation in theatre for, by and with people who have disabilities. Dr. Rickert has compiled a book, *Resources in Theatre and Disability,* which is essentially a print-out of the material in the computerized data bank.

Dr. Rickert does this work through a new organization, The Association for Theatre and Disability, which is a networking organization to maintain files and information on theatre and drama activities. This group (ATD), used to be part of the old American Theatre Assocation (ATA), which folded in 1986 for lack of money after 50 years. Dr. Rickert recently revived ATD as a national independent organization.

"We make a distinction between drama and theatre," he explained to us. "Drama is activities not necessarily intended for a public audience, like drama therapy, for instance, or creatives dramatics in a classroom. We include those forms, as well as theatre, which is for a paying audience."

CHAPTER FIVE

Puppets Guides Through the Looking Glass

Today the puppet is reaching more people
and serving more needs
than ever before in its history
—and it survives because it serves.
—GEORGE LATSHAW

"When I am working with a handicapped child often I will not use a stage at all so that the child and the puppet can play together. And frequently I will not let the puppet speak at all, unless it is absolutely necessary so that there will be a non-verbal exchange between the child and the puppet. I try to arrange some sort of activity between the two. If there are objects in the room that the child plays with, blocks or a xylophone or something, the puppet will haul it over and try to play with it, not always using the object correctly. This usually brings the child to interrupt the puppet and show how the activity should be done and this eases the child into generally showing the puppet how to do things and that is the beginning of a good relationship."

Explaining to us the value puppets have in bringing out the hidden talents and interests of disadvantaged children is one of the world's leading puppeteers,

George Latshaw, who hails from Ohio. When we talked with him he had just returned from China, where, as a member of a Very Special Arts team, he demonstrated how puppets can be used to advantage with children who have physical or mental impediments. He continued with his explanation of his work:

Puppeteer
George Latshaw

"For physically and mentally challenged children, the correcting activity gives them control over the puppet. And when you have control you have power. And if you have power you are functioning. You are superior. At first the puppet may evoke a waved instruction from the child's hand. Then the puppet can wave and you have started an interaction that can go on from there within a learning and artistic framework.

"When the child reaches the point where he can use a hand puppet on his own hand, the child may do something with his free hand and then he will have the puppet imitate the movement. Then you've got a sort of double learning situation in which one action reinforces the other."

We asked Mr. Latshaw if he could explain the powerful and enduring attraction puppets have for children. "I think it's because children are small," he answered. "They are small objects in a world of big objects—adults. Children's literature abounds in fanciful characters who are very small. The puppet is fanciful and small, so it immediately evokes feelings of identification and sympathy in the child. Children, you know, are able to give and receive affection from inanimate objects; just think of dolls. The puppet is a logical extension of this pretending and that's the advantage the puppet starts with."

Mr. Latshaw and his puppets began working with impaired children in 1977 and he says he had to learn as he went along about the special needs of the children. "In my early days I began working with blind and visually impaired children in Canton, Ohio. After one performance at a school for blind children the teachers brought a little boy backstage to meet some of the characters who had appeared in the play. The leading character was a boy of about pre-school age. And when the visiting child touched that puppet, my heart sank and I felt terrible. I wanted the boy to sense the warmth and softness that were in the character, but the material the puppet was made from was hard. I realized right then that for blind children, the puppets would have to be made of materials that matched the character's personality—hard for bad guys, but soft for good guys, and of course, soft for girl puppets, too. So for blind children I made a puppet, a bear, out of soft material, with soft ears and paws and buttons for the eyes and nose. The blind children can compare these shapes with the shape of their own nose and eyes and compare the shape of their own face with the shape of the bear puppet's face, and all of it is soft and inviting."

In his 1978 book *Puppetry: The Ultimate Disguise*, Mr. Latshaw tells why puppets have been popular since the dawn of civilization—and why they have particularly great value today for disabled children. He recounts how the first puppets were created by primitive peoples who wanted to communicate with their gods. The puppets were representations of the gods through which humans could address the deities.

"Primitive puppets were a link between the human and the spirit worlds. When the gods fell out of favor, the puppets remained, for they were experienced tour guides who could lead the living to whatever imagined world they wished to travel. I believe this is the secret of the puppets' enduring service to humanity. Puppets help us to see the unseen and to know the unknown in ways that are comic or comforting, according to our needs. Peter D. Arnott's marionettes evoke the essence of great theatre periods of the past. Bil Baird's marionettes simulate the moon walk for us to cover what the television cameras cannot show. Jim Henson's lovable monsters invite the young to venture into the unknown world of letters and numbers. Puppets today are doing what they have always done, providing a simulation device for exploring whatever inner or outer worlds the human mind can create."

Mr. Latshaw closed his discussion with us by revealing what his book's title means for those who work with handicapped children and wish to stimulate their imaginations by entering their imaginary worlds: when using puppets these adults are wearing the "ultimate disguise" which will permit them to accompany children through the looking glass.

A few years ago a special education teacher in Washington, D.C., had unexpectedly—and to her great surprise—exactly the experience Mr. Latshaw describes.

Kids on the Block
Barbara Aiello

In 1975, Public Law 94-142, often called "the mainstreaming law," ended the automatic exclusion of disabled children practiced by most of the nation's public school systems. At the time, a Special Education teacher named Barbara Aiello was teaching a class of disabled students at Sharpe School for the Handicapped, a public school in the nation's capital. One of them was Anthony, who had cerebral palsy and used a wheelchair. Soon after passage of P.L. 94-142, Ms.

94

Aiello decided it was time for 12-year-old Anthony to be mainstreamed into the public school across the street. She took him over there and settled him in.

"But a couple of weeks later, Anthony came back to my classroom," Ms. Aiello recalled. "He said, 'You can't ever make me go back there any more.' I was shocked and asked if he wasn't getting good grades. He said that wasn't the problem. 'No one plays with me. No one will talk to me. No one will eat lunch with me. I hate it over there. I want to go back to your class.'

"The situation put me in a real dilemma. All Special Ed teachers know there is a great deal of psychological capital to be made out of loving the kids that nobody loves and teaching the kids that no one wants to teach. It's so nice to have your kids love you and to give them a safe harbor in your classroom. But my other side was telling me that my responsibility to them was to prepare them for the real world and that meant to be able to function and compete in the real world, the majority of which is not disabled."

Ms. Aiello told Anthony he could come back, but only for a little while, until she figured out some way to make the fifth graders across the street more receptive to him. She realized he had to be pushed out of the nest, so to speak, but she also realized he needed some help along the way.

"As a Special Ed teacher I was accustomed to using puppets and it occurred to me that a puppet might be the way to help Anthony. For centuries puppets had been used as a non-threatening way to build bridges between people, so I thought they would be a good way to bridge the gap between disabled and nondisabled pupils. Communication becomes difficult because most parents tell their children that when they are around disabled people not to stare and not to ask questions. This enforced silence creates a knowledge vacuum in

95

which misconceptions and fear grow. The message children get is 'we don't talk about, don't even look at disabled people'—and because we don't, we begin to think there must be something real bad about them.

"But nobody ever tells us we can't talk to a puppet. In classrooms, puppets have an advantage over adults because they are a nonthreatening source of information and do not represent authority, although they have knowledge. Practically all children grow up fascinated by and loving puppets, so inadvertently I was capitalizing on the native curiosity and level of comfort kids have with puppets and attaching to those attitudes a very sensitive and sometimes threatening topic. Using Anthony as a model, a friend, Ingrid Crepeau, and I built a boy puppet, 11-year-old Mark Riley, who has cerebral palsy, and we made a wheelchair for him, too."

The teacher took the puppet to the fifth graders in the regular school. The puppet talked to the kids for a while about cerebral palsy. Then through the puppet Ms. Aiello asked if there was anything more they wanted to know. They began to ask the puppet—not Ms. Aiello—the puppet—all the questions they could not bring themselves to ask Anthony. They said things like, "There used to be a boy in our classroom who talked like you and wiped slobber from his mouth like this. How do you do it? How do you go to the bathroom? Why do you wear a hockey helmet all the time? Why does your wheelchair look like that?"

"I was astounded, Ms. Aiello told us. "From my experience as a teacher I thought I knew how powerful a medium puppetry was. But I didn't know anything. I asked myself why in the world these children would talk to a puppet and not to a real kid. After thinking about it a while, I realized that I had inadvertently taken a difficult and sometimes threatening subject and attached it to the native curiosity and degree of comfort children feel with puppets. They were able to set aside the threat of disability long enough to chat about it with a puppet."

Through Ms. Aiello, puppet Mark Riley gave simple, direct answers to the questions. He did not beat around any bushes. He told the children, for instance, that he did not have enough control of his muscles to write with a regular pencil so he did his homework with a large crayon, and sometimes instead of writing, dictated his work into a tape recorder. He explained that his hockey helmet was to protect him on the occasions when he fell out of his "cruiser," as he called his wheelchair.

"We had a one-hour session and that was enough to change their attitudes," said Ms. Aiello. "After it they wanted to meet Anthony. Kids came up to me as I was leaving and said, 'If you're Anthony's teacher, why don't you bring him back over here?' And when he did return, some of them said to him, 'There was a puppet in here who looked like you and he had CP. Do you have CP?' They now had a bridge over which to set up a conversation. I was amazed at the impact the session had, just amazed."

The experience inspired Ms. Aiello to make more puppets. The next was a blind child, the third a deaf one. Then she received a warning from a teacher friend.

"He told me I had better start making some nonhandicapped puppets. I asked why, since there was epilepsy to do, and cancer, and prostheses and a whole lot of other disabilities. He said, 'If you keep making just handicapped kids, you are going to recreate in modern times the old concept of the freak side-show at the circus. What you need to do is to model relationships between disabled and nondisabled children.'

He was right, of course, so my next character was nondisabled Melody James, a little black girl. And we have added more nondisabled characters since then."

Today Ms. Aiello is no longer a practicing Special Education teacher. She devotes herself to running The Kids on the Block, a group that now numbers 32 puppet characters who perform in 27 presentations developed and scripted by Ms. Aiello and her staff of 26.

Nondisabled children are not the only ones to benefit from the puppet shows. "Our biggest fans are disabled children—because they see so few representations of themselves. Disabled people on TV or in the movies are often made out to be super heroes. In contrast, our puppets are just regular kids, with ups and downs, hopes and fears, and they are seen in average, everyday situations."

Ms. Aiello and her group began as teachers and performers and grew into creators of educational materials. After a while they decided to be a private business, to make The Kids on the Block a going concern without federal or state help.

"We had to do that," explains Ms. Aiello. "Our chances of survival were greater that way. We did not want to be dependent on what government people think is sexy this season. One year it's neat to back Native Americans, the next year they back the elderly, etc. We couldn't survive in that atmosphere."

Buyers of the puppets are school districts, civic organizations, state departments of education and the like. Along with the puppets goes a kit containing scripts for the shows, training cassettes for new puppeteers and meticulously researched resource information about the disabilities the puppets represent. They now include a badly burned girl, a child suffering an emotional disturbance as a result of abuse, a Vietnamese boy in conflict over cultural differences. The puppets deal with 24 topics in all, including emotionally disturbed children, siblings of disabled children, children with epilepsy, asthma, diabetes, as well as the issues of child abuse and teenage pregnancy. The newest addition to the roster of problems which the puppets address is AIDS. The puppet and script have been undergoing development and field testing for the past 18 months. The AIDS victim is a 25-year-old woman who has been married for five years to a man who was an IV drug user and contracted the disease from a shared needle. His wife, Natalie Gregg, then contracted the illness from him. She discusses the many misconceptions people have about AIDS and the matter of safer sex.

"We don't sell puppets who have disabilities," explains Ms. Aiello. "We market a program, a curriculum, on disability. If you want to buy cerebral palsy, for instance, what you will get is the character Mark Riley and his nondisabled friend Melody James, a book that contains all the scripts for shows, as well as all the questions that kids commonly ask, along with the answers, and you will get followup activities, discussion questions, learning- center activities, instructions for simulations and instructions for creative dramatics so that children can take on the role of the character they have seen and finish an open-ended story. These followup programs build bridges between the fantasy world of the pupets and the real world of disabled and different children. We also sell a videotape that shows people how to operate the puppets and we have regional training sessions a half-dozen times a year."

Ms. Aiello's style of puppetry is the Japanese form known as Bunraku. The puppets are about three feet tall and dressed realistically, with real eyeglasses, braces or prostheses. The puppeteer stands behind the puppet, dressed in black, but in full view of the au-

Diane Dupuy, founder and artistic director of Famous People Players, with her troupe and three of the life-size puppets they use in their black light shows.

Raeanne Rubenstein/Telephoto 1987

dience. The fascination of the puppets is so great that after a few minutes of the performance, in the minds and sight of the audience, the puppeteer practically ceases to exist.

After the puppets perform and answer questions, they usually lead simulation activities to help non-disabled children understand the frustrations of having a particular disability. The effects of the muscle rigidity which often accompanies cerebral palsy can be experienced when children put a couple of pairs of socks on their hands and then try to button a shirt.

Troupes of The Kids on the Block are sponsored by organizations like the Junior League, the St. Louis Society for Crippled Children, the Georgia Learning Resource System, which serves the public schools of that state. There are now 900 such sponsored programs in 49 states and 14 other countries. The puppets are operated by volunteers who learn the craft of puppetry from the training materials and training sessions provided by The Kids headquarters in Columbia, Maryland. Some volunteers are physical therapy workers who want to learn as much as they can about various disabilities. While Ms. Aiello's early shows were designed to help children understand others who had disabilities, her motivation has broadened to help people of all ages accept differences between people.

Famous People Players
Diane Dupuy

In a surprising switch—or perhaps after you finish reading this section it won't seem so surprising—a troupe of mentally limited puppeteers has for the past 13 years been presenting top-drawer, commercially successful shows that have garnered rave reviews for their performances before sophisticated general audiences on Broadway, in the Big Rooms of the Las Vegas casinos, in Beijing and many points in between. They are The Famous People Players, a Canadian group whose home base is Toronto.

They are 13 puppeteers who manipulate life-size and larger than life puppets up to 18 feet tall. The puppets are painted with brilliant fluorescent colors that flash into blazing life when the stage is bathed in ultraviolet light, the so-called "black" light. The puppeteers, clothed from head to toe in black velvet, are invisible to the audience.

The show opens with the theme from *Superman* and the blackened stage suddenly bursts into wildly animated life: superman himself, R2D2, C3PO and Darth Vader. Steven Sondheim's "Send in the Clowns" brings a clump of clowns tumbling and galumphing across the stage. Later a zoo of fantastic animals dances to Saint-Saens "Carnival of the Animals" and the poems of Ogden Nash. There are performances by Barbra Streisand, Dolly Parton, Michael Jackson and other stars, whose life-size puppets are immediately recognizable. The show ends with a sketch under ordinary light so that the audience may see how the feats of near-magic are performed. Because of the size and weight of the puppets, as many as three puppeteers— always obscured from view except during this sequence—manipulate each character. At the same time, others rush about operating the iridescent props. The puppeteers are involved in a precisely coordinated ballet of intricate movements performed at high speed in which there is a high element of risk.

Says the founder of the group, Diane Lynn Dupuy: "They are working in complete darkness and they cannot see. It's a most dangerous technique—I can't be too strong about that. They have the hoods over their faces and on the front is just some black cotton mesh so they can breathe. The performers absolutely cannot see each other, get no hint of where the others are. The only things they can see are the black lights on the floor that show up brightly to them, though the audience can't see them, and the outline of their props. With people dashing on and off the stage at high speed there are collisions and we've had broken legs, broken shoulders, everything. It's as dangerous as walking a high wire without a net. That's why I'm thinking of doing a restaurant or some other interesting things with my people."

The performance that results from this hard work is remarkable, and there is nothing about the show that gives the audience even a hint that 10 of the 13 puppeteers are developmentally different. The Players was founded in 1974 by Ms. Dupuy, when she was working as a secretary for an organization that helps the mentally restricted. Like George Latshaw, Ms. Dupuy had been fascinated by puppets since she was a young child. She got started at age five or six when her parents gave her a puppet theatre. She has strong empathy with the members of her troupe for she was a slow learner who dropped out of school in the ninth grade.

"In school I stood out like a sore thumb," Ms. Dupuy recalls. "I had grown to my full height of five feet, seven inches by age 11 and that was pretty pathetic. On top of that, when the teacher fails you, as they often did with me, you also fail in the eyes of your classmates. Nobody wants anything to do with a dummy. It was very difficult.

"When I was in the seventh grade a new student came in and she was a lot more ugly than I was at the time. I was kind of relieved because everyone stopped picking on me and started picking on her. She had no friends and I ended up gravitating to her because it was the two of us against the rest of the school. She was an epileptic. We're talking now about 25 years ago and in those days we didn't have any education about handicapped people. We didn't know what an epileptic

103

was and to see that girl have seizures in the classroom, where her skirt would wrap around her neck, was absolutely horrifying. . .scary. Often the kids would laugh and scream because her pants were showing.

"Years later when I was working in Toronto I was asked to do a puppet show as part of a Christmas concert for mentally handicapped people. I refused because you heard so many horror stories about them and also because it reminded me of what people thought I was—the whole slow-learner bit. I just couldn't stand to be associated with all that. But a lady who worked with them leaned on me, so I did it. During the performance one of the audience had a seizure and like a flash I remembered the screaming kids and the panic in my class when my friend had her seizures. But here, everybody just got up quietly and did what they could to help. At that point I began to wonder just *who* was retarded."

After this experience Ms. Dupuy started working with developmentally impaired young adults. She suspected that they had creative abilities that others could not see, and which deserved to be encouraged. She decided she would train people who were viewed as being only minimally trainable and she would offer them a structure that would encourage them to be independent and to excel. Being a theatrical artist herself, she naturally looked in that direction to see what they might do. She felt the young people she was working with were capable of doing high-level theatrical work, but she knew that the physical appearance of some would prevent them from succeeding on the commercial stage. Then it occurred to her that if they could master what she could teach them about puppetry and then perform in black light, they could have a theatrical future. For in black light, while they would be onstage, they would not be seen. In 1974 she got a

$25,000 grant from the Canadian government as seed money to start The Famous People Players.

It took a year for the puppeteers to perfect the first five-minute number. When the grant ran out, Ms. Dupuy and her new husband, Bernard, used their wedding money to support the project for the next three years. Everyone Ms. Dupuy knew, and quite a few she didn't know, told her it was a ridiculous idea that would never work. And sometimes she thought perhaps they were right. After all, the concept that an untrained 24-year-old who had failed at everything she had tried—except puppetry—could take a group of undisciplined mentally handicapped young adults and turn them into a highly organized, first-class professional theatre group seemed unlikely, to put it mildly.

The first skit that came together in finished form, after many buckets of sweat and tears, was a puppet of Liberace playing the piano while candelabra, fur coats and jewels dance. It ends when Liberace, his wide grin unaffected, floats up above his piano and soars off the stage. Once her company got its act together, Ms. Dupuy began hounding Liberace's manager, Seymour Heller, to get the pianist to see the show. At one point she even threatened to lie down in front of Liberace's limousine. Mr. Heller, who now sits on the Players board of directors, says with a smile, "She clamped her teeth into the seat of my pants and never let go." Liberace came, saw, and was conquered—and he did *not* know the puppeteers were handicapped.

"I felt that if he knew he would have come just out of sympathy or it would have turned him off," Ms. Dupuy recalls. "I didn't want him to come to see it as a freak show. I wanted him to see it as a professional theatre company."

The ploy worked. Liberace liked the show so much

that he asked the troupe to make its American debut as the opener to his act in Las Vegas. That performance was a success.

"Going home with them afterward," says Ms. Dupuy, "I wouldn't have recognized them as the same people. They had achieved something remarkable, and they were so proud of themselves. They were so much more confident." They were such a success in Las Vegas that Liberace kept them on for eight seasons. "He was a wonderful, compassionate man," says Ms. Dupuy. "But he did not ever want to hear about us being handicapped. He always said he did not hire us because of that. He hired us because we were good, he kept telling us, and if we stopped being good he would kick us out."

The band of 13 puppeteers, supported by a backstage staff of 20, tours six months of each year, so the Players, all now in their thirties, have had to learn to meet and deal with a wide variety of strangers: stagehands and other theatre technicians, journalists, photographers, theatre executives, fans. Though most members of the troupe cannot read, of necessity they have had to learn how to use public transportation and to handle money. The path to these cultural enrichments occasionally has a disconcerting twist, however.

"We spent many, many hours over a period of months teaching them money," Ms. Dupuy recalls ruefully. "In Canada the different denominations of bills are different colors, so we taught the troupe to memorize the colors to know how much each bill was worth. And, wouldn't you know it, just when they had the Canadian colors down pretty good, we're off with Liberace to Las Vegas, where all the denominations are the same color. It was a nightmare, with hotel people complaining that my people were handing over hundred-dollar bills to pay for a cup of coffee! These kinds of things are always happening to us."

During rehearsal Ms. Dupuy is demanding, very demanding and to get troupe members to do what she wants she does a lot of shouting and arm-waving. She has no hesitation in pointing out Players' errors, and in a loud voice. If you were to watch a rehearsal you might very well come away with the impression that she is perhaps too tough on her young people, who are not as quick to respond to direction as average young performers.

"That you shouldn't be tough with them because they are handicapped is a widespread myth among those who work with people who have limitations," Ms. Dupuy counters firmly. "When they fail, you are supposed to shake their hand, pat them on the head, congratulate them for trying, and tell them, 'That's Ok, you'll do better next time.' Well, in the real world that just doesn't happen to you or to me. People pay good money to see us and theatres expect to make money when we do a show and my people have to understand and cope with the fact that if we fail in performance we will be out the door—pronto!"

"We don't mind when Diane is tough," asserted a troupe member. "She has to be tough. Diane is like a football coach. She has to push on the Players to get them to win. Being tough is the only way Diane will get a good show from us."

When Ms. Dupuy drops the veneer of toughness, for that's all it is, the mutual affection between her and her Players is apparent. Asked to explain the nature of their relationship, she thought for a long moment, then slowly mused, "They trusted me and I trusted them. Each of us was a step on a ladder that supported somebody else to climb up. We all held hands and we walked in the dark. We trusted each other and we loved each other. And that is how we got to where we are."

To an outsider it is apparent that affection is the glue

that holds the little band together. The intensity of their devotion to each other comes through strongly in the case of Renato Marulli, who is now 33.

Renato has a disfiguring large cherry-red birthmark that covers much of his face. "I had a hard time looking in the mirror," he says. "Because of this birth defect I didn't want to see myself. I got depressed." Years ago he used to rush off the stage to avoid curtain calls during which the audience would be able to see his face. Offstage he avoided people and social situations and was pretty much of a recluse. One night during the troupe's early days he learned that Ms. Dupuy was having a miscarriage with her first pregnancy. Renato is almost entirely blind and had never taken a subway before. But he walked up to strangers to ask directions and got on the subway that night, found the hospital, found the front desk, found the room.

"He pulled back the drape from around my bed," Ms. Dupuy recalls, "And he said, 'Diane, I'm so sorry.' I had lost my baby only a few minutes earlier and I had a sudden vision that at that moment my child was reborn in Renato. Ever since then he has been very protective of me. Everybody in the company looks up to him. He's really the company's godfather. He's an incredible man. . .incredible."

These days Renato stays on stage for the curtain calls and applause. Ms. Dupuy says that like him, all the Players have overcome their handicaps and are leading normal lives. But when we asked her to connect their improvement with their practice of puppeteering she declared she disagreed with the thesis of this book.

"I have to be honest with you," she told us. "It's not the art form at all. The key to it is integration—integration into society. They have to get on subways and busses and deal with people. When we were with Liberace they had to communicate with all his staff and when we were at Radio City in New York they communicated with the Rockettes. In China they walked on the Great Wall and met people there and talked with them. They're out there all the time, traveling, meeting, talking. When they were children they were led to believe there was something wrong with them and that they could never overcome it. Nobody believed in them. What The Famous People Players did for them was to surround them with a lot of encouragement and confidence, along with giving them plenty of opportunity to practice what they were learning, plenty of opportunity to get out and about with people. And we pushed them to do more and to do better. Yes, we pushed them a lot. It's not art, it's integration. You see, I could have opened a restaurant with this group and got just the same results.

"Another thing that helps is that this is not a segregated project, with only handicapped people around. I'm against segregated projects. Three of our onstage people have no problems, neither does any of the 20 people in our support staff. So the Players see, talk to and work with role-model people every day, the office manager, the business manager, the public relations person and they go to restaurants together and have lunch together. It's integration that has developed these people; that's the key."

Putting Ms. Dupuy's convictions into practice, the Players give benefit performances and donate money to help other groups. After their Broadway run, they donated $100,000 to organizations that aid the handicapped. But they insist that none of the projects be segregated. They make donations only to groups that integrate impaired people into society.

"With what we do we cannot take on a great number of people," Ms. Dupuy explains. "We're very limited because of the dangerous technique. But there's a great need to provide jobs for people like the Players.

Some people who see our show come and tell me they want to start a black-light theatre like ours. But I tell them black-light shows are not the answer. They can never provide enough jobs. I tell them, 'You have to look beyond black light and give these people jobs in your community.' I tell the same thing to the big corporations. If they would stop giving money to projects like ours and instead start employing these people they would be more effective and do more good. People like the Players make great workers. They're loyal and trustworthy and they'll work ten times harder than most normal persons."

Ms. Dupuy does not attempt to keep the Players permanently attached to her apron strings. Following the prescription she gives other organizations and the corporations, she encourages her people to learn other skills. During the half-year or so when they are not touring the group pays for training programs. They had considerable success with cooking classes. As a result of these, one former Player graduated with a diploma in French cooking and is now the assistant chef at a prestigious restaurant at Toronto's Eaton Center, the largest shopping mall in Canada.

Her work has brought Ms. Dupuy a passel of awards. In 1981 she was named B'nai Brith Woman of the Year. In 1982 she received the Canada Medal, the nation's highest civilian award. For innovative achievement in the arts she was given the first Ernest C. Manning award in 1984. She was the first Canadian to receive the Vanier Award, given by the Library of Congress.

How can one adequately sum up the myriad accomplishments of this admirable and intriguing company of puppeteers? That task was ably done by a newly enthralled fan who wrote a note of thanks to the troupe:

"As you move around in the dark, you turn on lights in our heads. Thank you." (signed) Alan Alda.

CHAPTER SIX

Visual Art
When Insight
Marries Imagination

There is a spirit deep in me
That clamors to be free
It cannot talk but tries to show
What is truly me
Truly, truly me.

That spirit roams the world
In search of beauty free
When I take colorcrayon in hand
'Tis that spirit guiding me
Drawing sets it free.

There is a spirit deep in me
That clamors to be free
When I take colorcrayon in hand
The drawing sets me free
Truly, truly free.

—*JOY BRAND*

National Institute of Art and Disabilities
Florence and Elias Katz

A couple who have had long experience in helping disabled people to express themselves through visual art are Florence Ludins-Katz, a painter, and her husband, Elias Katz, a retired clinical psychologist. They have been operating art centers for people with mental limitations for better than 20 years, which gives them the status of pioneers in the field.

Together they founded the Institute of Art and Disabilities in 1984 in Richmond, California, which is across the bay from San Francisco. This is the fourth art center the couple has founded in Northern California. They intentionally set up the earlier centers as demonstration projects to prove that disabled people could produce high-quality art work and be benefitted by doing so. As each center became successful, the couple turned it over to others and moved on to set up another center elsewhere.

A quarter century ago, through Mr. Katz's profession, they saw how developmentally disabled people in sheltered workshops were condemned to menial, repetitive tasks. The psychologist and the artist were appalled. "These poor people were performing the most mindless, boring tasks," Mrs. Katz recalls. "They had jobs that were too low for normal workers, or things that could be done cheaper by humans than by machines—folding papers, pulling out staples. Terrible." Knowing what they were seeing was wrong, the Katzes also knew they had to do something about it. They began in 1973 by teaching the basics of art to three disabled people in their home in Berkeley. In 1982 they set up their first free-standing art center, Creative Growth, in Oakland. Subsequently they set up Creativity Explored in San Francisco, and Creativity Unlimited in San Jose. These centers are serving as models for about ten others that people are developing around the state.

"When we started the first center we were told that we could never make it," says Florence Katz, "that the people didn't have the ability, that it was an impossible dream. But to the contrary, we've found in these people—some so severely retarded they have no speech, no communication whatever—that when you give them time and love and encouragement and materials to work with, they function well. It might take a day, it might take a year before we see anything happen, but eventually we do. Every day brings break-throughs. Every day brings surprises. For 20 years now we have been fighting to make people understand, to look at the proof we have that people who are developmentally disabled and who have failed in everything else can be wonderfully successful in art. Their art is absolutely amazingly beautiful.

"I have never found a developmentally disabled person who doesn't know they are different, and they are miserable about it because all their lives they have been teased, made fun of, made the butt of cruel jokes. But with us they find acceptance. If you ask 'what do you do?' they will say, "I'm an artist.' They feel a tremendous sense of pride in that. This is what my husband and I and the teachers are working on. It is not only art."

There are 120 artists currently at the center, ranging in age from young children to the elderly. The oldest student at this writing is 73, but there is no upper age limit. Most of the artists—which is how they are referred to—are developmentally disabled because California's Department of Developmental Services pays for their instruction. Without such state support, the Katzes say, they would not be able to operate. People with other disabilities are admitted on full or partial scholarships to the extent that the center's finances permit.

"As far as I know," said Dr. Katz, "every state pays for programs for developmentally disabled adults in what are called Activity Centers or Development Centers or such. These programs can be used as funding mechanisms for art centers, which we have realized here in California and we now have about 10 art centers that are supported in this way. But it's a constant battle for us to keep the money coming because the state people aren't really convinced our programs are worthwhile. When it comes to the disabled, the buzzword among government people is *employment*. Many of them would rather see our artists working in fast-food restaurants, where, by the way, they would need more counseling, supervision and support on a costly one-to-one basis than the people in our center need. Lots of the people in the Department of Development Disabilities don't understand art and don't understand the value of what we do, so we have to battle every day to try to get them to understand that art is a legitimate profession for everybody. When they deal with us, the government people don't talk about art. They class us officially as a "Day Activity Center."

Like many others who engage disabled people in the practice of art, the Katzes are adamant that what they do is not therapy. "We are not art therapists," Mrs. Katz declares. "We don't view art as therapy. We know that recreation comes from art, education comes from it and that therapy also comes from it. But we definitely do not use art as a therapeutic tool. What we are interested in is the enrichment of human life."

The center has four teachers, Mrs. Katz and three other professional artists. Each teaches a different art form: painting, sculpture, printmaking, and crafts. "They are highly skilled people," explains Mrs. Katz. "They don't come to us through Special Education. When we hire someone, they must be a practicing artist so that they can transmit the artistic feeling to our people and can accept our people's work."

Larry Stefle is the sculpting teacher. "What impresses me about their art," he says, "is the spontaneity of it, the uninhibited quality. These people are not worried about getting into galleries. They just do what they want to do."

There are no formal classes at the center. Instead, the procedure is based on a concept the Katzes refer to as an open studio. Each person chooses what he wants to do and works by himself. The function of the teachers is to offer support and guidance as needed and as the artists request.

The artists, who are supported by Supplemental Security Income, are brought to the center each day in minibuses. It costs about $120,000 a year to run the center and they usually come up about $20,000 short, which they make up through foundation grants, rummage sales and an occasional gift. The Katzes take no salary, living on Dr. Katz' pension.

The Katzes feel one of their important achievements is the redefining of some venerable ideas about the relationship between talent and IQ. "The young woman who painted that swan can't even write," pointed out Mrs. Katz. "What that tells me is that the IQ level assigned people is false. IQ tests a certain type of intelligence, but not the whole person. In our society we tend to take a person and cut him up in pieces. I say we should look at the whole person. I have had so many people tell me they don't believe our students can do the work. Even when they see our people, they don't believe it, not until they are actually in the room and see the art being produced. The development of a person through art is the most remarkable thing. For 20 years we have been fighting for recognition that developmentally disabled people are gifted, that everyone is gifted if we don't knock it out of them. Unfortunately, in this respect the schools are the greatest criminals. I was an art teacher in New York City high schools for 15 years, so I know."

Sculptor
Alonzo Clemons

There are always around the world a handful of people whose abilities are conclusive proof of Mrs. Katz' assertion that mentally limited people often are artistically gifted, sometimes spectacularly so. One of these is Alonzo Clemons, a 30-year-old black man in Colorado who has spent most of his life in institutions for the retarded. The doctors say he has the mental ability of a six-year-old. But what Mr. Clemons also has is a marvelous talent as a sculptor. A leading art gallery in Denver has sold hundreds of pieces of his work, some of which have brought prices in five figures.

Mr. Clemons sculpts only animals—what animals! Collectors, one of whom has bought more than a dozen, describe them as "stunning. . .glorious. . .almost alive." Completely untrained, he works in hard sculptor's clay, using no tools, only his fingers. It is awesome to watch him work. When he completes the torso of a snorting bull, he will lay it aside, pull a piece of clay from the large ball on his workbench and mold it to the shape of a handsome leg. When he attaches it to the torso, the proportions and the angles are perfect.

Most trained sculptors would take days to calculate the proportions, trying them out in drawings of poses and muscles. Only then would they begin on the difficult model. Mr. Clemons never sketches; his fingers simply "know" the correct proportions. Figures that would take other sculptors weeks to complete, he does in an hour, or at most, several hours. He very rarely has to correct a shape or a muscle; nearly always his first molding is the right one. He has a photographic memory and does not need models in front of him when he is molding his gorgeous pieces.

Alonzo Clemons, inspired sculptor, with his work, "Charging Bull." Duopatina 11" long × 7-1/2" high, cast by Art Castings of Colorado.   Driscol Gallery

Painter
Richard Wawro

Another gifted artist who is very similar to Alonzo Clemons is 35-year-old Richard Wawro (pronounced Vavro) of Edinburgh, Scotland. The physicians regard him technically as having the mental development of a six-year-old. He was born with cataracts in both eyes and had surgery for them, but the doctors said he would have badly impaired sight all his life and he is now legally blind. When he was three he was autistic—withdrawn, screaming, given to repetitive motion. He did not speak until he was 11. His parents, however, rejected the advice to put him in an institution.

When he was quite young he began spontaneously to draw with crayons and he now works with oilbound crayons. These resemble a child's crayons, but are more difficult to work with and produce more sophisticated results because they permit layering of colors.

Mr. Wawro today produces magnificent landscapes and streetscenes, and like Mr. Clemons, produces his work from memory. He can draw in exact detail places and scenes that he saw months and even years before. His process also resembles that of the Colorado sculptor in that when he makes the first stroke on a blank sheet of paper, in his mind he already can see the finished product and knows every subsequent stroke he must make. There is no trying and changing. His eyesight is so poor that when working he must hold his face three or four inches from the paper.

The Scotsman's work was first shown when he was 17 and his pictures were an immediate success. His work has since appeared in hundreds of shows in many countries and he has traveled the world to attend ex-

Richard Wawro from Edinburgh, Scotland, demonstrating his drawing technique at a VSA Festival. His painting, "The Island of Scilly," is from the private collection of Richard "Cactus" Pryor. VSA

hibits. Several thousand of his works have been sold. They are owned by such collectors as Britain's Prime Minister Thatcher and Pope John Paul II, who has two.

People like Mr. Clemons and Mr. Wawro pose a mystery for specialists in intelligence—and for everyone else. Unable to live independently or to care for themselves and not comprehending a great deal of the world they live in, yet they produce mighty works of art that are the envy of many highly skilled artists of "normal" intelligence: how?

Dr. Harold Treffert, a psychiatrist who specializes in trying to unravel the puzzle, has taken a stab at an explanation. "We are a series of intelligences and artists like these actually have a single island of intelligence." Some others guess that their extraordinary talents are related to the division of functions between the two hemispheres of the brain and that a defect in the left hemisphere results in exaggerated development of the right hemisphere, where the perceptual skills are located. Bernard Rimland, another specialist in this phenomenon, thinks one answer may lie in the powers of concentration of people like Mr. Clemons and Mr. Wawro. He says, "They can shut out—as a result of some impairment in their intellectual capability—the kinds of distractions that affect other people and devote 100 percent of their mental energy to the task at hand. Their minds are like electronic calculators, or tape recorders, or cameras. They capture the specific details of a picture, or the notes of a song, or the sequence of a mathematical process, and can then play it back or manipulate its details with astounding fidelity."

But other mentally limited people who do not have such stupendous abilities can, in a nurturing and learning art environment, develop their latent artistic talents to a surprising degree. An example of such development is 23-year-old Leslie Sylvester, who was trained in a class for art aides in the Katz art center just outside San Francisco. The Katzes set up the course in September 1985 to train aides for jobs in nursing homes, public schools and day-care centers. Ms. Sylvester is the first member of the class to get a job. Since September 1986 she has been working eight hours a week in two nursing homes. It's her first paying job. "It's an experience for me to get out there, get a job and be nice to people," she smiled.

The course, which is funded by the city of Richmond and IBM, has had difficulty recruiting students. Most of those who have applied would not have been able to hold a job. The class is taught by Sondra Cohen, a painter, who ascribes the recruitment problem to "a bias against art," among social workers, "a feeling that art is fun, but not a real future for anybody." Cohen said most developmentally disabled people who can work are shunted into fast-food restaurants or given a job with a mop. "But many are talented," she said, "and they could earn money as art aides." Of nursing homes, Cohen said, "They very definitely need us. None of the homes we approached have art programs."

An important activity for the center is arranging exhibits of the work of its artists. They have mounted 47 shows in the past three years. They go into galleries, museums, public buildings, hospitals, schools, "any place that is willing to go along with us," says Dr. Katz. A twin exhibit of works and photographs by Judy Dater showing the artists at work in the Katz center traveled throughout California in 1985 and 1986. The exhibit was funded by a $10,000 grant from the California Arts Council, the Department of Developmental Services and the Department of Mental Health. These statements are from the exhibit catalog:

121

"Open to all disabled artists in the country, the response was overwhelming. Due to lack of space only a few of the works could be selected. No concession was made because of the type or severity of the artist's disability. The quality of the art speaks for itself.

"Some of the works are by professional artists, others by amateur artists. The works are diverse by almost any standard, but all have in common a meaningful and creative vision worthy of recognition. This exhibition is indeed a triumph of the human spirit."

The catalog includes statements by each artist. Here are two:

Michael Richard, 32, a trained professional artist who is an instructor at the Katz center:

"My assemblegraph prints are conceptual pieces that require an explanation. I spent the first 25 years of my life as an active able-bodied person. When I suffered a spinal-cord injury in 1977, I felt dejected, like a piece of discarded human trash whose usefulness was gone.

"In my prints I employ articles that reflect who I am and where I live. The main subject is the carburetor gasket which when used with the assemblegraph technique turns into a magical thing of beauty.

"These prints are highly symbolic to me. The abstract beauty of these prints make me reflect back to those early desperate days as a quadriplegic, the feeling of uselessness just as the gaskets outlive their usefulness. As the gaskets have been reborn, I have been reborn."

Roger Maberry, 49, studied at the Art Institute of Boston, the Massachusetts College of Art, and the University of New Mexico:

"The process of making art is as simple and pure as the act of playing, and since the child within me loves to play I always have been in the process of making art. It is the only thing I know how to do well. It is the only time I am honestly and solely myself. All things are possible in art; there is no right or wrong. I don't think I could live without doing my art- making, for I would have no sense of purpose. My art work is the total, true expression of myself, body, spirit and mind. It is my only reality, and it validates my very state of being.

"Since the onset of my oculo-cranio-somatic neuro-muscular disease I have been forced to try new ways to do my art work. This has enabled me to be more creative in trying materials and developing new art techniques. No longer am I stuck with just the traditional way of making art. I can no longer work for long periods of time on my art. However, I do it more often."

Asked her view of whether disabled artists should have their work segregated into special exhibits or should be integrated in general exhibits with the work of other artists, Florence Katz said she has mixed feelings. "I hold two opposing views at the same time," she told us. "On the one hand I am against segregating the work of disabled artists. I feel all art should be shown together, no matter who produces it. On the other hand, I'm an advocate for the disabled so I must work to get them recognition. As a practical matter, we do both. We have our own shows and our artists also submit in regular juried shows."

While the exhibits are important for giving the disabled artists an ego boost and for informing the public about them and the center, the Katzes know that the greatest ego boost for artists is when their work sells. Until now their work has sold in small quantities, helped by the exhibits. But recently the Katzes acquired funding to hire a marketing specialist to boost sales. When sales are made during an exhibit in a gallery, the gallery gets 50 percent of the sale price, the artist gets 25 percent and the center gets 25 percent. The center's commission is used exclusively for the benefit of the artists as a group—to take them on trips, to pay for framing, to buy equipment for the use of all.

The Katzes lecture extensively on their work. When we talked to them they had just completed a series of 20 lectures throughout California that were funded by the National Endowment for the Arts. They also organize conferences on art and disabilities. One such assembly was a four-day session of meetings and demonstration workshops held in October 1984. The group discussed an interesting agenda of issues:

> What is the place of disabled artists in modern society?
> How have disabled artists been regarded throughout history and what contributions have they made?
> Does the stigma of being disabled prevent an artist from reaching his full potentialities?
> Are off-beat and innovative creative ideas threatening to the establishment?
> What are the implications of "labeling" to the artist and to society?

Another element of the prodigious efforts Dr. and Mrs. Katz make on behalf of disabled artists is the writing of books. In 1983 they published themselves a 235-page instruction manual, *Art & Disabilities*, on how to organize an arts center for the disabled, how to set up and teach the classes, how to get funds and how to get the public interested in the work of the center, and scores of other concerns of importance to anyone who wishes to follow in their footsteps. A short segment from the book will give you a feel for the practical, nuts-and-bolts approach they take to their subject:

Art is best produced in an environment which stimulates the imagination. There should be a studio atmosphere of freedom to create which is nonjudgmental and noncompetitive. The space should be large, light, uncrowded and flexible, with no constraints of preconceived neatness and conformity. Floor should be of concrete or linoleum which are easy to maintain and pose no cleaning problems. Every section should be easily accessible to all persons, no matter how severely handicapped.

Experimentation with many tools, materials and ideas should be encouraged. An abundance of inexpensive supplies should be available: paper in a variety of sizes and colors, cardboard, wood scraps, wool, clay, different types of chalks, crayons, paints, etc. There should be no limitation on the use of color, materials, style or size of working.

Students should be able to make the choice of working on tables, on the floor or on easels, since different projects can best be accomplished by using different props. Only the artist himself knows what is comfortable for him.

Learning through experience, especially in the arts, is essential for each person in order to explore and develop his own individuality, his own ideas and his own unique methods.

It is essential to have trained art teachers, since in every art student's growth there is a time when he feels the need for instruction in techniques which only a well-trained art instructor can provide. The staff is there to help the student develop according to his own needs and inclinations. The teacher's job is one of stimulation and encouragement and to be available when needed for teaching special skills. Never should the teacher become the dominant force. The learning of specific techniques should be considered secondary to the joy and desire of creating and to the excitement of discovery and fulfillment of the creative act.

In this type of environment where limitations are minimal it may at first seem that students will abuse their privileges. For those of us who have worked with students using this philosophy we find the exact opposite happening. People enjoy what they are doing. They stay with their work and are motivated to investigate. They progress at their own rate. They learn to respect their work and the work of others. They learn the possibilities and limitations of the materials they are working with. With each student's involvement in his work and his sense of accomplishment, with the interest of the staff and the community in the student's accomplishments, he develops and changes. Why it happens we do not know, but it happens. He begins to take control of himself. There is a difference when discipline is imposed by external forces such as the staff and when discipline evolves freely from the person's need for order and organization in dealing with a free environment. His self- image and self-esteem as well as his ability to deal with his own problems grow and he feels himself a person of worth. This feeling transmits itself to his total personality and to his total functioning as a human being.

There is no one way of developing and structuring an Art Center. Each will be individual according to local needs, funds available, types of disabilities served, ethnic make-up of the students, the expertise, experience and philosophy of the Board of Directors, the Director and the staff. Some Centers concentrate on one of the arts such as painting; while others include several arts. *The basic commonality is the focus on creativity, the belief that each person can grow in many dimensions, can enjoy himself and can produce work of high artistic quality.* [Emphasis in original]

In response to requests from teachers who wanted information on how to conduct art classes for disabled students, the Katzes in 1987 published a 75-page classroom handbook titled *Freedom to Create: Philosophy and practical experience enabling teachers to stimulate creativity in the visual arts for disabled students*. The Katzes explained that since the specialized art teacher

126

is now almost extinct, they wrote their book for regular and Special Education teacher who wish to bring art into their classrooms. The authors have convinced the Richmond school system of the value of art in the classroom and will be working with the schools to implement the concepts and techniques they put forth in their book. If you would like either book, see Appendix 1.

The Katzes bubble over with enthusiasm, ideas and plans for the furtherance of their work. They want to form a mutual-support network of art centers like theirs, establish a gallery, mount traveling shows, set up an archive of original work, engage in research and in teacher training.

"A main reason we published our books," the Katzes explain, "is that we would like our work to serve as a model for others, to show others what can be done and to show them how they can do it too. We are anxious for this idea to spread. In fact, because they think our work has national significance, the Board of Directors has just added the word *National* to our name, so now we are the National Institute of Arts and Disabilities.

"We want to see the validity of this work recognized nationally, that what we've been accomplishing isn't just a California quirk. These things are possible throughout the whole United States. We'll give guidance and advice to anyone who wants to do what we've been doing."

Rehabilitation Through Photography

As far as handicapped people are concerned, the most overlooked of the visual arts is photography. It appears that only one organization in the entire U.S. provides photographic equipment, instruction and help on an organized basis to people who are disabled. In addition to being unique in its field, the organization also is one of the oldest, if not *the* oldest provider of visual art instruction to those with limited physical or developmental abilities.

Located in New York City, Rehabilitation Through Photography, Inc. has an ancestor. In 1941, a photographer and teacher named Josephine Herrick, a member of the American Women's Voluntary Services, put together a group of volunteer professional photographers and named them War Service Photography. They took on the job of snapping at New York's many canteens servicemen who were on their way overseas into World War II. The photos were mailed to the men's families with a note from the volunteer. Later, when the wounded began returning and faced long periods of hospitalization, Miss Herrick and her volunteers started teaching them photography as recreation. They designed and built an ingenious portable darkroom so even those who couldn't leave their beds could join in.

Medical people soon recognized the value of the programs as rehabilitation therapy. One of first of these was Dr. Howard Rusk, the noted specialist in rehabilitation who now heads the world-renowned Institute of Rehabilitation Medicine in New York City. For many years now, Dr. Rusk has been a sponsor of the volunteer photography group and the Institute he heads has one of their longest-running programs. Another sponsor is the famed photographer Yousuf Karsh.

Because of the success of its programs in the veterans hospitals, they were kept going through the wars in Korea and Vietnam. In later years they were expanded into civilian hospitals and institutions which serve the physically and emotionally disabled. To reflect this expansion into civilian institutions, the name of the group was changed to Volunteer Service Photographers. Quite a few people mistook the meaning of the name, however, and VSP found itself fending off a regular flow of requests from people who thought the group provided free photography at weddings and Bar Mitzvahs. In an effort to clarify matters, VSP adopted a slogan to accompany its name: Rehabilitation Through Photography. In 1983, deciding to end the confusion for all time, VSP promoted its slogan to the status of its formal name.

Rehabilitation Through Photography has a tiny staff. A full-time Executive Director, Jean Lewis, who has been with RTP for 30 years, and three part-time people, oversee and support at this writing 36 photography programs in 27 institutions. In these, 35 people were teaching and helping 616 adults and children. About half of the instructors are volunteers, the other half being staff members of the institution in which the program is located.

Keeping up with the changing needs of the times, RTP has just launched a program with an organization that is devoted to helping victims of AIDS. It also is just beginning an innovative program for people who are visually impaired. It has been shown in recent years that many psychiatric patients improve when they are given a pet as a companion and the director of the stress-reduction center at the Creedmoor Psychiatric Institute in New York State has come up with an original way of using that knowledge. Joining the pet program to the institution's RTP photography program, participants are being given pets to care for. Pets, of course, are outstanding subjects for the camera. It is hoped that each program will have a synergistic effect on the other, making it more effective than it would be by itself.

Nearly all of RTP's photographic equipment is donated and when the organization responds to a request for a program, they lend the requesting institution all the hardware—cameras, enlargers, etc.—that is needed. If the institution cannot afford to buy the paper and chemicals that are used up, RTP will provide them free for three months. "We have found," explains Director Lewis, "if a program is going to be successful and useful, we can see it within three months. Then we expect the institution to find the money for the supplies." As long as the program is operating well the RTP equipment remains with it on permanent loan.

RTP makes two demands on the receiving organization. They must send in regular reports of attendance and accomplishments to show that the program continues to be viable. And the program must participate in the annual picture contest which RTP runs. "This requirement," Ms. Lewis says, "is very important. Looking forward to submitting pictures for the contest provides people with a strong motivation to keep going in the program. They start working toward it months in advance and getting a picture shown gives them quite a feeling of achievement. We announce the winners and give small cash prizes. For many of the people this is the first time they have been publicly recognized for achievement."

RTP has numerous success stories in its files: elderly patients who have been roused from deep, chronic depression; people in wheelchairs with so little muscular control that they use a camera clamped to a lapboard and snap the shutter via a cable release held in their teeth; psychiatric patients who previously refused to communicate with others becoming able to express their feelings through photographs.

The principal of the Bellevue Psychiatric Hospital's school for emotionally disturbed children had this to say of the program's value: "For each student who has participated in the program to a greater or lesser degree, the camera has functioned as a window that permits them to look out into the world and gain new perspectives and also permits the professional staff to get glimpses into the private world of the student."

An assistant principal at the Robert F. Kennedy School day treatment program for profoundly emotionally handicapped students said this of the RTP program in the school: "Photography has provided an opportunity for our students to work in small groups, exploring their environments and translating their perceptions in a manner that is vibrant and dramatic. It also has given them an avenue to experience success in lives that too frequently are defined by failure...Stay with us; continue to embrace us with your support."

Ms. Lewis told us of some extraordinary experiences in RTP programs. She said: "Volunteers in our programs have told me repeatedly over the years that people in our darkrooms have had remarkable experiences as far as physical disabilities go. They'll go into the darkroom saying, 'I can't do this' or 'I can't pick up that, it's too hard.' But then they get so wrapped up in the creative process at the enlarger or the development tray that without being conscious of it they do things they thought they couldn't do, move muscles everybody believed they could not move. I don't know what that's all about, I only know I've been told many times that it happens."

This is the second time we've been told that. Bob Alexander of Living Stage described the same phenomenon in chapter four. When we first heard it, we thought it was a welcome, but isolated, phenomenon unique to the experience Living Stage was providing to its people. But having heard it now described for a second time, as occurring in a very different branch of the arts, we wonder if such happenings are perhaps more widespread, but have not been noticed; if possibly there's more to this arts-for-the-disabled enterprise than has met most professional eyes.

Throughout its 46-year history, RTP has limited its operations to New York City and its suburbs. However, if anyone wishes to start a similar program elsewhere, RTP will give advice and share its experience. An information package is available for the asking.

Electric Drawing Board
Jack Harvey

A problem for many disabled artists is that they are unable to rotate or reposition their work on a table or desktop without help from someone else. Also, easels on tables have a tendency to move around.

Jack Harvey of Manton, Michigan, an engineer and designer who retired from the aircraft division of the Eaton Corporation of Battle Creek in 1976, has come up with a solution for these problems. Having met a quadriplegic artist and studied his difficulties while working, Mr. Harvey designed an electrically operated drawing board that is proving popular with artists in several countries. The board is mounted on a cabinet on wheels. It allows rotation of the drawing board 360 degrees, both clockwise and counterclockwise. It is adjustable up and down and back and forth, making it possible for a person whose legs are in a horizontal position in a wheelchair to work comfortably. In the prototype he built himself, Mr. Harvey used a television antenna rotator from K-Mart and altered the control box so that it could be operated remotely from the wheelchair. He has since also designed an economy model without the cabinet.

The drawing board has attracted attention and has

been written about in Canada, Great Britain and China in addition to the U.S. One artist "blessed" Mr. Harvey for creating the easel. Something of an inventor, the engineer says the reaction to the easel has given him more satisfaction than anything else he has developed.

Mr. Harvey offers the plans for either design to anyone for the cost of reproducing the blueprints and postage. (See Appendix)

Electric Easel designed by Jack Harvey.

CHAPTER SEVEN

Networking
A Gathering Together

I just try to share a little bit of me. . .
I'm just one human being trying to find my way. . .
I guess that is what we all are trying to do. . .
just find our way. . .disabled or not. . .
As artists. . .as human beings. . .
as members of life. . .
With God's help and my special people. . .
maybe I'll find my way. . .
I'm sure of it. . .

—DEBBIE ALAIMO

An idea whose time has come is the concept of net-working by and for disabled artists. This concept is built on the belief that among the people most skilled and best equipped by experience to help disabled artists are the artists themselves. The networks are being built on the belief that while the help of people in the larger community is always welcome, the main thrust toward gaining general acceptance of disabled artists must be led by the disabled themselves. It is they who can prove that disabled artists are no different from other artists—and just as competent. The networks so far are few in number and very much in their infancy, but they hold promise for the future.

Disabled Artists' Network

One of the most active networks is the Disabled Artists' Network [DAN] which operates out of New York City. It was founded in 1985 by Sanda Aronson, who is quoted in Chapter One on the use or euphemisms for disabilities. This is her description of the Network:

> It's an information exchange and "living bulletin board" of disabled artists in the visual and sculptural arts. After becoming disabled I wanted to meet other disabled artists. The Disabled Artists' Network represents people with a wide variety of disabilities who practice different kinds of art. As disabled artists, we connect with each other and know we share the same core —*the art will get made.*
>
> We introduce artists to each other and exchange information about shows, competitions, galleries and opportunities for professional artists who are disabled. There are no dues or meetings. The price of membership is only a willingness to correspond and to share information. We have about 30 active members.
>
> We also work toward educating the general public and the arts community about disabled artists. We've noticed that organizations and agencies working with the disabled seem to be confused, as is some of the general public, whether disabled artists are *real* artists. We're working toward eliminating this kind of confusion and we would like to see the work of disabled artists gain more visibility. Disabled artists are innovative problem-solvers (an extension of the concept that making art is problem-solving).
>
> The Disabled Artists' Network is an independent organization and is not affiliated with any organization or agency. The Network has given me good fellowship, and through it I have become older and wiser in ways I would never have imagined.

There are a number of ways to measure how effective a network is. In the personal realm, the offering of simple human support and warmth helps to deal with solation and loneliness. Members' letters are the best evidence. One wrote from New Jersey:

"I'm really very grateful you've been there to write :o because, except for my brother, who has no real nterest in art, and my parents, I have no friends I can :ommunicate with at this time. I especially have no)ne here to offer me any support for my work and you've been able to fill in for that important gap in ny life."

A note from California, from Elissa Barlow, an artist who has had multiple sclerosis since 1980, contained similar sentiments. A realist painter of animals, she wrote that being able to correspond with a number of other artists is so "very rewarding, extremely helpful for me. I am able to share my burden with other artists, plus gain a lot of other information. Before, at times I wondered if I was the only one doing this."

Loneliness is a recurrent theme in the letters DAN receives. Another is that corresponding with the network and other members relieves them of the boring burden of having to constantly *explain* to able-bodied people "how they feel." Writing to each other, members report, they "don't have to explain all the time."

Another way to measure the network's effectiveness is by what it accomplishes for artists in the professional realm. In 1986, the United Cerebral Palsy Association planned a show of art—the first national one by professional disabled artists—and they turned to DAN for advice. Ms. Aronson suggested that because so few shows of this kind are mounted, it should be a non-juried show and open to as many submissions as space allowed. She urged UCPA to raise more money for prizes and for return shipping of the works submitted. Finally, she urged that no commissions should be taken for sales made at the show. The organization followed her advice in all areas.

Through the network, an engineer got in touch with Ms. Aronson. He told her he had designed a mobile, self-adjusting drawing board for quadriplegics. Ms. Aronson helped to achieve magazine publicity for the non-profit device and got the engineer and quadri- plegics in the network together. The drawing board is described in the previous chapter.

The network has brought together artists in the same field with similar disabilities who wanted to ex- change technical information on problem- solving. Says Ms. Aronson, "Matchmaking is my greatest sat- isfaction."

As part of their getting to know each other, DAN members have been exchanging biographies. We can think of no better way to impart a flavor of what net- working means to its members than to reproduce some excerpts from their descriptions of their lives and work.

Betty Edwards

I started painting in 1984 when I signed up for an acrylic landscape class. I had never thought I would be able to paint. Several months earlier, my husband bought me a drawing table. I had been drawing pic- tures from his hunting magazines. I always liked draw- ing but didn't think I was that good so I didn't do it on a regular basis until my daughter started taking art classes in high school. She was really good so I asked her to show me what she was learning in school. Learning the basic techniques for pencil drawing made my drawings much better.

I am mostly self-taught with the help of instruction books, art magazines, and talking to other artists. I took a floral-painting class and one three-hour work- shop also. Painting is an on-going learning experience to me. The more I learn about art, the more I want to learn. I just can't seem to get enough. I haven't limited myself to only painting landscapes. I want to try it all. I also want to try different mediums. I have done a few florals in pastels, too. I have sold 15 paintings.

My disability started in 1972 when I was diagnosed as having multiple sclerosis (MS). I had always been very active physically so this really changed my life drastically. I walked with a cane for about a year and then the symptoms seemed to disappear. I was back to normal. The only thing that wasn't back to normal was my attitude. For about seven more years I harbored feelings of self-pity and depression.

In 1979 another problem in my life caused me to join a self-help group. I got off of the pity-pot and began to live again. I came to an understanding of God that helps me get through the bad days.

In 1982 I married my present husband and shortly after my MS reared its ugly head again. I have experienced blurred vision, loss of 50 percent of the strength in my left arm and hand, numbness, loss of bladder control, fatigue and I am walking with a cane again. I haven't given up though. I live my life "one day at a time" and look to God for my strength and courage.

Vincent Tafarella

I started painting in 1968 as a hobby. In 1971, I was forced to leave my job as a furniture upholsterer and go on disability due to suffering from an inner-ear problem. It causes dizziness and a feeling of imbalance and vertigo.

All of my art works are made from mixed media, which include: plaster, acrylic paint, oil paint, modeling paste, sand, aluminum, water putty, wire and sculpmold, plus stain. Most of my work is done on plywood, some on canvas. My work is a combination of painting and sculpture and is three-dimensional. I like experimenting with different media.

I have been home due to this disability for 15 years and in all that time my work has been keeping me going. Each art work that I create is the best until I create the next one.

I have had an exhibit at the Kingsland House in Flushing, the Philip Jackson Fine Arts Workshop in Sunnyside, the Sunnyside Library and the Fresh Meadows Jewish Center Art Show, where I got an Honorable Mention.

Recently I have become involved with an independent living center which plans to start a gallery for artists who have a disability. The gallery will give disabled artists a place to exhibit work.

Ruth Urban

I'm surprised that art has become my mental salvation and physical work. As a child in the 1940's, drawing was just another thing I did for fun, along with reading or climbing trees.

I took an art class in high school. The instructor was stuffed to the eyebrows with 1950's "modern art" and taught us nothing. After a year of college I worked, married, and had four lively sons. I used my old pastels only for Halloween faces on my boys.

My health deteriorated in spurts and in 1974 I had to quit even a part-time office job. My husband and my mother (no doubt as sick of my frustration and depression as I was) sought to give me a new interest by buying me some acrylic paints and brushes. They created an expensive monster, as I found my need fulfilled. I managed to attend some very useful art classes before becoming more disabled, including one absolutely wonderful class that taught me previously unknown wonders such as negative space, the color wheel, etc. A new world welcomed me.

I now sell enough pictures to pay for my art supplies, have a big scrapbook of ego-boosting ribbons, and a whole room for my studio. My favorite medias are soft pastels and oils; people are my favorite subjects. I also enjoy doing landscapes, groups of people in their special settings (such as a wedding reception), and some still lifes.

My illness has, over the years, been mislabeled rheumatoid arthritis, thyroid imbalance, stress-induced potassium deficiency, and diabetes-induced. Presently it is nameless and consists of peripheral neuropathy of arms, back and legs with involvement of muscle and sensory fibers. There are some painful times, some falls, and the atrophy continues to spread. I also have hypertension and mild diabetes. My goal is to stay mobile as long as possible. I use a wheelchair away from home. In 1978 Social Security Disability reviewed my records (shortly after one of my sons was killed) and took away my pension. I continue to appeal.

In my paintings I can be anywhere and do anything I want. My goal in art is to combine reality, imagination, technique, and soul into the most complete image possible. I want the viewer and the image to share a feeling.

Debbie Alaimo

My work in the visual arts has been, and still is. . .a safe inner harbor. . .to weather storms. . .repair the broken pieces. . .to rest. . .relax. . .to cry or hide. . .to whisper. . .to SHOUT. . .to play. . .to express feelings. . . to celebrate. . .and REJOICE in my God. . .to explore and find me. . . ABLE and FREE!!! When I venture out into the sea of life, I try now to have God as my captain. It's then the journey holds meaning.

I must have been born that June of 1952, with at least a crayon in my hands, for I can't remember a time in my life that I wasn't creating a "MASTERPIECE"! I struggled to maintain the high grades expected of me, due to undetected dyslexia, however in the fine arts I prospered. Due to some life experiences, that need not be mentioned, I was mainly a loner. . .apart. . .from my peers at school.

The year 1982 found me married to a wonderful hubby and mom to two fine boys. I was a full-time mom learning new ways to live off of our land (garden). My oil painting blossomed and held an excitement to keep creating. We were very active in Boy Scouts of America, our church and family activities.

A few months after moving to Wisconsin, I sustained

a fall, that combined with being bodily struck by a car in 1979. I had back surgery. The damaged discs were corrected but I was left in chronic pain and partial use of my left leg. The idea of having to use a cane or something else, I refused to accept!!! Painting became a refuge. . .to hang on. . .to hide. . .to work out feelings. As my denial grew and the inner war raged, my work became forced.

I was encouraged to turn to my artwork as a career. The realization of myself as a professional was and is still a new concept. Yet as one way of life was ending under protest. . .this new one began. It was after my first Christian Art Show in 1984, I realized I had come home. To a world where I belonged. . .but never dared enter before.

I received a grant from our state dept. of Vocational Rehab. to attend the Univ. of Wis. at Waukesha. I was 34 and a freshman, (part time) in the beginnings of a degree in fine arts. College was a means to help me reach my full potential as an artist. It was while at school that I found a Doc. who finally gave me some answers. Not ONE did I like. . .very possible M.S., along with painful inflammation problems in my joints, including costochondritis (inflamed cartilage connecting ribs to breastbone) and a few minor conditions. Along with my prior back problem. . .I couldn't fight any longer. . .nor deny. . . not any more.

It has been a couple of months now and acceptance is not easy. But I'm not fighting "it." I have gained much support from my family, pastor, school faculty and some good friends. . .I'm making it. . .slowly. . .my activities have been cut way down. . . I'm semi homebound. . .by the Grace of God I can still function in some areas outside of family, school and my artwork. I'm still active in church and B.S.A., but in less demanding positions. Some friends have left my life as a result of my conditions. . .Letting Go can Be So H A R D. . . . .

I've been given rainbows too. . .my career is advancing. . .I'm gaining more exposure. . .shows are coming up. . . I'm exploring new media. . .special people have come into my life. . .I have a lot to learn about the business part, like galleries etc. . .My paintings and sculptures have gained a new freedom. . .I'm on my way. . .an artist. . .I found me ABLE and FREE!!!

Judy Nunes

I can't remember not drawing or trying something with art. My art is like a part of myself, an arm or leg. Without my art I'm lost. At the times I've been unable to paint I've felt adrift from myself. I can almost say that drawing and painting is a way of centering into myself and pulling my impressions of the world out. I'm also a struggling poet, and when all else fails, I've found writing as a means of coming into touch with my feelings and sharing intimate thoughts with others close to me.

I'm 33 yrs. old and was raised in the Los Angeles, Calif. area. I was raised in a home surrounded by art, my mother being an artist and instructor. I attended local schools, and as a senior in high school won a scholarship to a life drawing class at the Art Institute of Los Angeles. This experience really made me feel special, I was an "ARTIST."

My art schooling was never really formal. I attended classes at Junior Colleges here and there. In 1974 I started to work exclusively in oils, and shortly thereafter left the Los Angeles area, heading for the wooly woods of Humboldt County, Northern California.

I can really say that finally being on my own and so far from my family helped me to grow and explore my own style and ideas. I had always tried so hard to copy my mother's work, her subjects and ideas, that now I had to think on my own. In moving to Humboldt I was really able to experience rural America for the first time. The faces of the people around me has always been my number one subject. Even in the expansion of my subject horizons I still come back to portraits time after time.

Five years ago I was diagnosed as a borderline diabetic and put on a diet control program. I was just adjusting to this lifestyle when in Jan. 86 I was hospitalized for a back injury. (Slipped disc with a hairline fracture, scoliosis, and a spinal malformation due to a birth defect.) After a bunch of nasty tests, and because I was found to be so drug sensitive, surgery was cancelled. The Drs. decided that I would have to adjust to a limited lifestyle, and have physical therapy to maintain muscle tone. PAIN. . .is an everything [sic] thing to be endured one day at a time.

I'm 99 percent homebound and paint in a prone position. I've, with therapy, achieved the ability to lie on my stomach for short periods of time. In this manner I'm able to do my watercolor washes. I work over washed in Berol Prismcolor pencils, and in this way achieve the vibrancy of color I wish. I keep my colors separate in an old Coca-Cola crate by my side.

I've shown in many local business and Art Festivals and in Sept. 85 had a one-woman show that was well received. I belong to local art organizations.

At a very low point in coping with my disability I wrote to DAN, and having the understanding and sharing has been a boost. It is helping to give me a purpose for this day-to-day struggle to endure.

Each of my days starts with the little voice inside my head saying

Lord, this is Judy again. . . . .

Joseph Crivy

One of my earliest childhood memories is that of being sprawled on the floor, filled with fascination and pleasure, as I drew in crayon upon a sheet of paper. I would close the bedroom door as I drew for I relished drawing as a solitary act and wanted no interruptions from the other members of my household. When I started public school my artistic ability was noticed and in my third-grade class the teacher had me create a mural in the back of the room while the other members of my class were doing their lessons. I chose to make a picture of a seascape with Chinese junks drawn in pastels. My parents, hearing word of my artistic

144

ability, enrolled me in an art class for children when I was eight years old at the Brooklyn Museum Art School. I went to the children's class for many years and when I was sixteen years old I enrolled into the high school drawing class which worked with nude models. Seeing nude females for the first time filled me with awe, the beauty of women captivated me, but I also discerned a certain power in the naked woman which intimidated me. Regardless of these divergent feelings, I loved drawing nudes.

When I graduated high school I had won two scholarships but chose to go to Cooper Union Art School, after passing their entrance exam. I majored in Fine Arts at Cooper Union and graduated in 1954. Cooper Union was a three-year school, from there I went to Yale University's School of Fine Arts for two more years to obtain my Bachelor of Fine Arts degree, majoring in painting. After graduating Yale University with my BFA I returned to Brooklyn and worked for a display company painting figurines for Christmas displays that were going to be used by department stores. After working six or seven months, I was drafted into the U.S. Army in December of 1956. I served most of my military service in Fort Hood, Texas, working in the Corps of Engineers the first portion of my service. Later my job category was changed permitting me to work as an army illustrator. The army let me out three months early to return for my Master's degree at Yale University. I stayed at Yale for one year and took my second year out of residence, returning to New York.

In New York I worked in the textile field as a colorist and as a designer for two years. In the evenings I would go several times a week to sketch classes drawing from the nude model. In 1961 a close friend who taught at Pratt Institute told me of an opening there for a figure-drawing teacher. I applied for the position and was hired by the evening art department. Gradually I was hired by other departments in the school. I was drawing and painting at this time, trying to improve my skills as a realist. In 1962 I realized that parts of my

145

body came within my field of vision. I began painting environments including my body in an attempt to make the viewer, kinesthetically, feel that they were me. This was a time that innovation was an important ingredient in art—but my paintings met with little success. After teaching seven years at Pratt Institute as a per diem instructor without a contract or rank, I applied to the University of North Carolina at Greensboro for a job and was hired as an assistant professor where I taught graduate and undergraduate courses. When I was in Greensboro I spent two years working on a series of etchings on a theme of metamorphosis, images that were part human and part animal. At this time, a three-year-old love relationship was terminated and a few months later, in February of 1974, I suffered the first of many mental breakdowns. I was given the rest of the semester off to recuperate after which I resumed my teaching for a few more years. I was turned down in my bid for tenure. After seven years of teaching at the university, I moved from North Carolina to Washington, D.C.

In D.C. a former student and myself shared model expenses and would draw nudes in my studio apartment. After several months of working together my former student moved out of town and I could not manage the expenses of hiring models alone, so my drawing sessions came to an end. A short time later I suffered one of several more mental breakdowns. During my first breakdown in D.C. I destroyed forty of my paintings, hundreds of drawings and almost all of my etchings and etching plates. After several more hospitalizations I was sent to Area A, a mental health day care clinic. I attended Area A for three years, the last year part time as I obtained a CETA job as an administrative assistant for the National Museum of American Art. The Reagan administration terminated the CETA program in April of 1981 and a few months later I moved to Brooklyn close to my parents. Living alone I suffered severe depression for many months. I eventually enrolled in the Postgraduate Center for Mental Health for about a year. During that year I resumed my art working, creating large ink drawings on a metamorphosis theme which was completed in November of 1984. The drawings have been admired for their artistry but tend to turn people off by their content. I have not done much drawing since then but feel that am getting ready to embark on a new series of drawings. These will be intimate portraits of individuals I have a close relationship with which will attempt to convey their inner spirit as well as their outer physical characteristics.

I am now in intensive therapy at Beth Israel's Medical Center and in a few months have learned more about myself than in ten previous years of counselling. It has been determined that I'm a manic depressive and I'm on lithium.

I desire more contact with artists, those in good health and those who are disabled, for companionship and for artistic stimulation.

Joyce Pies

I began majoring in art in college in 1971 and after one-and-a-half years, I moved and attended an art school in Denver, where I gained more knowledge of the many techniques, materials and differing concepts of art. I developed a wide variety of styles, which range from Super-Realism, the Abstract, Surrealism, Avant Garde, to other modes of art.

Back then, and even now, I enjoy using very meticulous, tiny details in some work, but also, am able to use very simplified and loose techniques in other projects. My works have included abstract and realistic portrayals of people and natural objects, such as rocks (agates, crystals, etc.), shells, feathers, mountains and animals; but I also like mechanical and hard-edge structures as well and incorporate some of these ideas into my works.

At the art school I also studied commercial art and accumulated projects for my portfolio, which I later revised, eliminating some and adding others, in an attempt to continually keep it up to date.

147

In 1975 I decided to get a degree in another field and went back to college to major in Special Education. I did not become disabled until 1983 and so back then I did not realize that a background in Special Ed would directly relate to my future in other ways than teaching. While in college, and later, after receiving my degree in Education, I gained experience in working with individuals with many different types of disabilities. I often integrated my skills as an artist into techniques of teaching which were involved in "Art Therapy" according to each one's individual needs, pleasures and capabilities.

My present illness is diagnosed as peripheral neuropathy, with constant and sometimes severe pain, partial numbness and tingling in my hands, arms and shoulders, head, back, hips, legs and feet, so it is practically a total involvement with the body and there is much difficulty in mobility and also with any use of the hands. Since the pain and symptoms increase with any movement, everything gets worse as the day goes on and it is a great task to do any sort of artwork, writing, gross and fine motor control involving the hands. It is out of sheer force that I do anything at all and do get too carried away with my work as I still have difficulty in knowing my limitations. Now I use similar techniques in art as before, but mainly on a smaller scale and with simpler use of the materials.

I continue to try to be as productive as I physically am able, often far extending my own capacities, considering my condition; but being an artist has allowed me to carry on and develop more of a fine acuity of all of my senses. I am interested in communicating with other artists to learn about their styles and techniques, ways in which they handle their tools and materials, and also to learn about their goals and accomplishments. I am thankful toward Sanda and others involved in originating this organization and wish to gather and maintain an alliance in the network.

Sanda Aronson

For me, making art is like having an itch that must be scratched. When I was 10, I knew I would be an artist. I already felt special because I had an odd first name and an unusual birthday, February 29th, Leap Year. However, most of my recognition as an artist has come since I have been disabled.

I have severe allergic asthma. Many substances trigger asthma attacks, including chemicals, natural substances and strong odors. Chemicals include petroleum products, plastics, tobacco, perfumes—did you ever think about how many products are perfumed?—cleaning materials and print. Natural substances include animal danders, pollen, molds, dust. Strong odors include cooking smells, such as garlic. It makes my daily life extremely limited. I have been print handicapped for about four years. That means books, magazines, newspapers—anything printed—triggers asthma attacks. For printed matter, I must rely entirely on xeroxed material. However, the amount of xeroxed material I can tolerate is small,limited almost entirely to my correspondence and the DAN material I mail out. For access to information, I must rely primarily on audio cassettes.

People frequently make me ill because of odors on their clothing. I endure a great deal of physical isolation. I continue to become more sensitive. I also have a muscle disorder that has not yet been diagnosed, plus Hashimoto's thyroiditis. I have stamina problems and exotic symptoms.

Having an invisible disability means people often do not believe I am ill because they don't see anything. Now that I need a wheelchair to get outside, it's a more visible disability. Since June 1985, I have been almost entirely homebound.

I feel enormous psychic pain at having a chronic illness with limited physical abilities and having a creative life is balm and salve for my soul. But at the same time it is painful to have to limit the scope of my work, not to be able to carry out some ideas and projects

149

because of my various disabilities. I am angry and sad that so many limits are placed on me. I'd rather have more choice.

Despite the limits her illnesses place on her, Ms. Aronson maintains an output of art work and a large volume of correspondence with members of her network and with members of the general art community. During 1987 she had work in these exhibitions—none of them shows limited to disabled artists, but all juried shows open to any artist:

National Sculpture Conference: Works by Women, Covington, Ky.

National '87 Small Works Exhibition, Cobleskill, N.Y.

Tenth Annual U.S. Print & Drawing Exhibition, North Carolina. In this she received the Purchase award for her woodblock print.

Tenth Annual North Dakota National Juried Exhibition, Minot, N.D.

1987 Artists' Society International Exhibition, San Francisco.

Matrix Gallery, Sacramento: Transcending Confines, Miniatures.

Emerald City Classic VI '87, Nepenthe Mundi International Competition, which she won first place, sculpture.

Also in 1987, and previously in 1986, the Pollock-Krasner Foundation gave her one of its grants for artists of merit who are in financial need.

Ms. Aronson is on the Artist-in-Residence Board of the new *Access to Art* program of the Museum of American Folk Art in New York City. She has been a Board member of the Women in the Arts Foundation in New York City. She is a member of the New York Artists Equity Association.

She is listed in *Who's Who in American Art*, in *Who's Who in the East*, and in *Who's Who of Emerging Leaders in America*.

Ms. Aronson was graduated from the State University of New York, Oswego, in 1960, then went on to study art.

I took a few courses in collage with Paul Pollaro at the New School in New York, then courses in ceramics at Tulane in New Orleans. Later, in Denver I also took ceramics, then a couple of classes at the Art Students League in New York. I am mainly self-taught.

Sanda Aronson, founder and executive director of Disabled Artists' Network, in her studio. Ralph Schwartz

After a decade of working in clay in my own studio I had to give up clay because of my allergies to dust and mold. It took me a few years to stop working in clay completely because it was painful to give up a material I loved, but each time I handled the clay I got very sick.

Because I like experimenting and finding solutions to problems, I began my evolution of materials. I'd already developed a one-firing clay method and gleefully made pots with thin bottoms and figures with hollow insides or bottoms so I could avoid spending time trimming. I love challenging the rules. I now make assemblages and collages. Throughout my clay decade, I did collage, so it was natural that after clay I would build upon collage, my first love, and work 3D collage. Assemblage is 3D collage to me.

Artists often ask me where I get my materials. When I was a walker I collected found objects on the street. Now, friends shop flea markets for me and collect street finds, such as a car grille and broken adding machines. *The Long March* uses adding-machine parts. My son gave me toys he'd outgrown and I used some in *Play is Work/Work is Play*.

As I've become more physically disabled, I've begun to mine the humor in my subconscious. Although the assemblages are formal in structure, I like adding wit as counterpoint. I've also dealt with some serious feelings in my first disability-theme work, an asthma xerox collage.

Association of Foot and Mouth Painting Artists Worldwide

For many of us it would seem inconceivable that an artist could paint or sculpt without hands or without the use of their hands. The fact is, however, that a great number of artists turn out highly proficient work—work that sells—while not having the use of their hands or arms, or both. They hold their brushes, styluses or carving chisels in their mouths or between their toes.

Some were talented artists before they lost the use of their hands, others learned their art after they became handicapped. Many do extraordinary work. Genevieve Barbedienne, for instance, was born in France without hands or arms 63 years ago and paints by holding the brush in her mouth. The excellence of her work was recognized a few years ago when the prestigious French Society of Art, Science and Literature awarded her its bronze medal. Another recipient of the same medal is Louise Tovae-Annick, 54, who lives in Switzerland. She paints with the brush held in her toes, which have become more skillful than the fingers of most of us.

Erich Macho is a 62-year-old Austrian who was born without hands and paints with his feet. Graphologists are puzzled and awed by the fact that no matter whether Mr. Macho writes with his left foot, his right, or with his mouth, the structure, quality and assurance of his writing is unchanged. Fifty-seven-year-old Charles Brown lives in Ireland, near Dublin. His arms and legs have been paralyzed since birth and he paints with his left foot. He has written a novel, *My Left Foot*, which has been translated into several languages.

These artists and others like them have banded together into The Association of Mouth and Foot Painting Artists Worldwide. The organization's purpose is to enable its members to avoid both pity and charity through helping them to become self-supporting. The organization markets the work of the established artists among them and also helps art students without hands who show talent to pursue their studies. Currently the group has 54 artist members and 98 student members. The Association was founded in 1954 by Arnulf Erich Stegmann, 76, who lost the use of his arms and hands during a siege of polio and now paints with his mouth. As a youth he was an outstanding student at several art schools in Germany and by the time he was 20 his work had been exhibited in several countries. He paints just as assuredly in oil with brush or spatula as he does in water colors. He also does pen and crayon drawings and lino and wood cuts. Several countries have bestowed honors on Professor Stegmann for his work in art and for promoting the social welfare of handicapped artists.

In 1961 an American branch of the world organization was set up in Buffalo and there is an office in Canada. The American group is named the Association of Mouth and Foot Painting Artists. A member of the American group is Neita M. Kimmel of Catawissa, Pa. Born with cerebral palsy, Ms. Kimmel, 66, began painting at age 14. She expresses well the determination of these artists in the face of their apparent helplessness. "People used to look at me," she recalls, "and say 'Oh, poor thing, she can't do anything.' But one day something happened. The little girl who couldn't do anything was painting by holding the brush in her mouth."

The artists retain ownership of their original works, but they grant reproduction rights to the Association, which sells copies and a line of notepapers, wrapping papers, greeting cards and calendars displaying the art works.

Deaf Artists of America

Another piece of the contemporary explosion in organizations and services by and for handicapped artists is Deaf Artists of America (DAA). Like the Disabled Artists' Netowrk, DAA was founded in 1985 and now has more than 300 members. It is the brainchild of founder and Executive Director Tom Willard of Rochester, New York. He explains that the concept of DAA arose from a simple question: why is there no National Gallery of the Deaf? While the National Theatre of the Deaf had existed for almost 20 years, there was no comparable institution for deaf visual artists.

"I was teaching photography at the National Technical Insitute for the Deaf in Rochester," he explains, "when I began to talk with people there and in the Rochester community about the possibility of setting up a gallery. Not only would such a gallery provide a showcase for the work of deaf artists, but it also could provide a variety of other services.

"Talks with experts, however, convinced me that to do a gallery first would be putting the cart before the horse. The advice was to first develop an organization for deaf artists and leave the gallery for later. It was good advice and now, with the gallery remaining an important goal, we are putting our efforts into building a strong support network to meet the needs of deaf artists throughout the country.

"Since our founding, people have been writing to ask if DAA is open to performing artists, writers and other kinds of artists. I want to make it clear that DAA is for deaf artists, no matter what art form they work in. At the same time, however, being new, we have decided to focus initially on the visual arts. There's good reason for this decision. There are more than 40 deaf theatre groups in the country, while organizations for deaf visual artists are practically nonexistent. I also want to stress that DAA is for all hearing-impaired artists, whether they are totally deaf or less than that."

Soon after its founding DAA began publication of a quarterly newsletter. There are plans to convert this into a quarterly magazine, *The Deaf Artist*, which will contain feature articles and news related to deaf people and the arts. A number of other programs are in the planning stage:

A directory of deaf artists which will include biographies of the artists and samples of their work.

An annual convention of deaf artists.

Publication of calendars, posters, T-shirts and other items featuring the work of deaf artists.

Financial support for talented deaf artists, including fellowships, scholarships and loans.

Competitions and an art contest for deaf school children.

Services for members, such as legal and business advice, group health insurance and employment referral.

Discounts for members on art supplies and publications.

"As a deaf artist myself," Director Willard explains, "I'm well aware of the frustrations and challenges we face on a daily basis. It's not easy being an artist, and being deaf makes it that much more difficult. This organization is designed to improve the opportunities available to America's deaf artists, a development that benefits not only the artists themselves, but our society as a whole."

Wright State University Arts Conference

For ten years Wright State University in Dayton, Ohio, has had the Center for Arts for the Disabled and Handicapped Person on its campus. It exists to provide training for teachers and others involved with assisting the handicapped with art, to publish resource materials, to provide a variety of arts programs and to hold conferences of professionals in the fields of human service and the arts. The Center staff is planning a national conference for artists who have disabilities to be held in Dayton in June 1990.

The purpose of the five-day meeting is to look into problems between the general population and the community of disabled artists, such as stereotyping and problems of physical access to museums and other display areas, the public relations efforts needed, earlier introduction of disabled people to the arts, and a number of other topics.

The educational core of the meeting, however, will be a comprehensive career development workshop designed to help disabled artists toward making a living through their art. Recognized professional artists who are disabled and who have "made it" will lead the workshop and will present hands-on information about working with talent and literary agencies and retail outlets. The leaders also will deal with how to overcome physical, emotional, attitudinal and social barriers that stand between many disabled artists and success.

Also at the workshop will be educators, career counselors and arts administrators who will discuss career options in the arts, support services such as job banks, professional associations and specialized networks like Disabled Artists' Network, and how to deal with the disability in interview situations.

CHAPTER EIGHT

Poetry Reflections from the Soul

*The pencil lets you say
what the mouth does not*

—*A PSYCHIATRIC PATIENT*

N.Y. Hospital - Cornell Medical Center
Karen Chase

Karen Chase, a poet, spends her days in what might seem to most of us an unusual locale for a poet—the wards of a large mental hospital. In the New York Hospital Cornell Medical Center in White Plains, New York, she helps patients who have serious mental illnesses to construct poems. Writing poetry often empowers them with the ability to come to grips with the overwhelming rages, fears and other destructive emotions that they have been unable to deal with in any other way. The results for some patients have been excellent—gaining ability to communicate, a skill which is of great benefit to working their way back into the community.

If the promising early results of this poetry experiment hold up under the necessary rigorous analysis, peer review and requirements for replication, it will be a major new development in the treatment of mental illness, including schizophrenia.

The medical people have joined with Karen Chase

in a research project to try to discover why and how the act of poetic creation brings such benefits to patients. "We are trying to discover why it is that mentally ill persons can function well when writing a poem when they are at a loss at just about everything else," Ms. Chase explains. "And why it is that this limited area of functioning sometimes begins to carry over to other parts of their lives?"

An indicator of how the project has matured and found acceptance is that during 1987 Ms. Chase began a formal lecture series for fourth-year students in psychiatry at the Cornell University Medical College, a step that represents an important change in the training of medical students.

In psychiatry there is a discipline known as poetry therapy. It bears about the same relation to poetry as physical therapy does to the kind of creative dance engaged in by Anne Riordan and Bruce Curtis or the kind of physical, participatory theatre practiced by Bob Alexander's *Living Stage*. Ms. Chase is adamant that what she practices is poetry, not poetry therapy. "In poetry therapy," she says, "people write things that can look like poetry and maybe there is even sometimes a rhyme, but the writing deals *directly* with the subject—if you hate your mother today, you write it down. But that's not the stuff of poetry, which always deals *indirectly* with the subject matter."

"Creative acts are healing," Ms. Chase notes. "People have known this for centuries, so, perhaps my contribution really is to have rediscovered something very old. But, while music and dance have occasionally found their way into a hospital patient's day, the writing of poetry has not. And I mean the writing of poetry in the classical sense. I am not a poet therapist and my work with patients is not structured toward achieving therapeutic values. While the *effect* of poetry writng may be therapeutic for some people, I don't believe he *goal* of poetry should be to achieve therapy. I have never made claims about what it will do. What I do is each poetry writing and what happens, happens.

"The poems patients produce are viewed by everyone connected with the project as potential works of art, not tools for psychological probing. I have stubbornly resisted hospital pressures for me to become a clinician. I am a poet and only a poet. The medical staff never see patients' poems unless a patient wishes to show them. And I report to a patient's treatment team only in the capacity of a lay person closely involved who is passing on her observations. I am not a *member* of the treatment team. So our research project will, I believe, be a rich collaboration of a poet, psychologists and psychiatrists, each with different viewpoints."

Karen Chase has had long experience at doing what she's now doing. For five years she was in the Poets in the Schools program of the Connecticut Committee on the Arts. In her workshops she discovered that the best work was done by the students who were most rebellious and most emotionally stressed. The experience gave her a clue that as a poet she might possess a key to a healing process and she moved to a more difficult school, working with delinquent and emotionally disturbed girls. There she began to glimpse just how potent for disturbed people her work could be. "I got very wary," she explains, "of how powerful it was for people beleagured by strong emotions to have them writing poetry—and I had never taken even one psychology class! I felt a real need to work in a place where there were greater safeguards than in a girls school. I wanted to work in a teaching hospital, where I could begin to learn some psychology."

So after a year at the school she moved to her present hospital situation. In her seven years with the hospital, Ms. Chase has worked with about 150 patients in both individual sessions and in workshops. The patients were in the hospital between one and three years and have a range of diagnoses, including schizophrenia. They are between 16 and 45, with most in their twenties. While working with others, her own poetry output has been published regularly. Having the instincts and drive of both a poet and a teacher, she explains that as a poet she values her own writing and as a teacher she wants to bring the same experience to others.

"When I began at the hospital, many medical people regarded poetry writing as a frill," she recalls, "a somewhat charming and interesting activity for patients. But many of the physicians now see the patients' writing of poetry as a unique way of making contact with otherwise unreachable human beings, and as a bridge toward their developing a more solid inner self. It's also true that it wasn't until I had been working with patients for some time that I started to realize just how potent the work is."

While poets sometimes build castles in air—after all, isn't that part of what a poet is expected to do?—physicians rarely do, and their technical assessments of what has been occurring in Ms. Chase's poetry workshops have a gravity and heft that lend them high credibility and authority.

Dr. Ann Appelbaum, Chief Physician for two of the wards in the Division for Extended Treatment Services, where the workshops take place, has written:

> Since many of our patients are described as "borderline personalities," they experience manifestations of identity diffusion, and a major task of the hospital treatment is to help these people consolidate a sense of identity. We believe we have seen this happening in

162

several patients who now see themselves, not as "authors," "writers," or "poets," but as people capable of expressing important feelings with ideas through the medium of poetry, in such a way as to be recognizable to others. Since "identity" is a complex psychological issue having to do both with feelings about the self and with social recognition and confirmation of the individual by others, poetry that is shared with and read by other people can constitute an element in a person's sense of identity. One young man, for example, who joined the workshop a year ago, at a time when he felt utterly worthless, and took pride in nothing that he did, now has come to value his poems, thinks (legitimately) of seeking publication, and produces poems of steadily increasing excellence from week to week. His discovery in himself of the capacity to write will have been a significant aspect of his improvement in the hospital. There are other instances, undramatic but still important, of patients "finding themselves" in the process of writing poetry.

Another observer of the result of the poetry process that has been occurring on wards he supervises is Dr. Richard Munich, Director of the Division for Extended Treatment Services. He wrote:

> These wards treat seriously ill and regressed patients who have abandoned traditional means of communication and in some cases have lost the ability to use fundamental aspects of language. It is our belief that substantial breakthroughs in making contact with these patients can be achieved through this modality by providing a transitional means of communicating and articulating otherwise disconnected thoughts and feelings. It is our hope that the research will serve to document this phenomenon and lead to a more widespread promulgation of this technique. It is important, however, that this not be thought of as poetry therapy, but rather as the imparting to patients of important linguistic skills.

"Cindy, who had been hospitalized on and off for many of her 32 years, rarely left her room," Ms. Chase recalled. "I met with her once a week for eight months. When I approached her about our working together, Cindy remarked that she disliked poetry. I explained that I could offer her a chance to write, read, and talk about poetry and that I wished to work with her. She consented, probably because of a wish for personal contact. After numerous meetings, during which we talked about many subjects, mostly related to writing, I read her *The Poems of Our Climate*, by Wallace Stevens. After saying a bit about the poem, indicating that she had quickly grasped the sense of it, Cindy said, 'It's condensed. It's how I think. I don't like how my mind works and poetry is like that. It reminds me. It scares me.'

"During our meetings, I read Cindy my own poems and those of other poets. She read me her writings, which she described not as poems, but lists. They were carefully constructed series of words on which she worked for hours at a time to come up with the exact five- or six-word list that satisfied her.

"When she was being discharged we had our final meeting. She remarked that she still did not like poetry, but was glad we had worked together. When I asked why, she responded, 'I learned about how I think.'

"Cindy's earlier comments suggest her sense that there is a relationship between the particularly condensed language of poetry and her form of disordered thinking.

"When patients hear or read a poem, whether or not they have been exposed to poetry, their interest is usually awakened. One reason might be that they are witnessing language used in a way which is familiar to them. The familiarity might arise from the fact that

Karen Chase, poet, a staff member at New York Hospital, Cornell Medical Center.

poets, like patients, have not been bound by conventional speech; they have taken liberties in order to communicate material which is otherwise difficult to communicate. By the unconventional use of speech, poets are often set apart from what is viewed as the ordinariness of others. Severely ill patients feel they are different from others and some appear to find comfort in identifying themselves with poets. And, perhaps for narcissistic people, they can imagine themselves above others, along with the poet. Assuming then, that poems ring true to patients, why would writing poetry be a suitable arena to explore? Poems have an accepted place in the world, in contrast to people who speak in an eccentric way. A poem which employs unconventional grammar construction and made-up words, as long as it communicates, is considered acceptable, whereas a person at the grocery store who talks to the checkout person in an odd way is not considered acceptable. One aim of poetry is to communicate with others while maintaining an individual personal stance. If made-up words are used, that is fine.

"If patients can be encouraged to express themselves through writing personally and accurately, no matter how unconventional that expression may be, and taught to embrace the goal of communication, they have made a step into the world away from isolation; thus a large step toward recovery.

"Poetry is condensed, with thoughts and feelings expressed in sparse wording; few words echo many meanings. Patients in severe distress often speak in a condensed way and their speech can be puzzling. By being shown how their sparse speech can make contact in a poem, they are offered a way to make use of it. The following poems were written by the same patients. In the first, condensation obscures meaning. In the second, condensation enhances meaning:

1	2
Where, I couldn't say	*adjoining the man*
how, either	*a tree*
it was very intense	*washed*
that's for sure	*white*
"enough said"	*seldom ceasing*
	a dance
	of parts
	like branches

"Because poets and some psychiatric patients use language in similar ways, they have a common meeting ground. This makes the writing of poetry particularly suitable for the psychiatric patient's experimentation. Poets use certain modes of expression in a controlled way to intensify communication. It is the work of the poet in a psychiatric hospital to teach the patient how these modes of expression either succeed in making contact or fail, and to gain mastery over them. I believe our work is showing that experimentation with language through writing is healing.

"Poetry offers the protection of a veil, a metaphor, to dare tell the truth. As Oscar Wilde said, 'A man is least himself when he speaks as himself. Give him a mask and he will speak the truth.'

"Take this simple example. A fourteen-year-old boy who had behavior troubles at school was referred to an outpatient day hospital. In The Poetry Workshop he was given a stone and asked to write a poem pretending that he was a stone. He wrote:

> *I am a stone on the beach*
> *Some throw me in*
> *Some throw me out*

Then he wrote: That's why I like being a stone. He proceeded to cross out 'I like' and wrote 'I don't like.' I asked which words he wanted. He said he didn't care. He was asked which words he meant. 'I don't care,' he said. Then he was asked, 'What did the stone mean?' With gusto, he wrote: 'That's why I hate being a stone.'

"One may have good reasons not to tell the truth. Writing poems affords a person an opportunity—though not a necessity—to tell the truth in an indirect way.

"Poetry, like other arts, is based on transformation,

turning one thing into another. As Tennessee Williams said, 'I write—why do I write? Because I find life unsatisfactory.' Or, as a patient/poet said to me 'I like writing poetry because you turn a toad into a train.' When one is in a state of despair, the chance to transform that despair into a form which contacts and affects others is helpful.

"Poets and psychiatric patients share common ground, though while the poet tries to reach people the patients often are people who remain distant from others. By its nature writing aims to make contact, so through writing, the isolated patient has much to gain. Poets and psychiatric patients also share a flexible use of language and vision, but while the poets are freed by their exercise, psychiatric patients most often are hampered by theirs.

"If patients are given the opportunity to write poems, using the twists and turns of their minds toward acceptable and communicative ends, the endeavor can heal. Most, if not all, psychiatric patients are badly wounded in their self-respect, and writing poetry validates a person's worth in their own eyes and in the eyes of others. Anything that legitimately heals these wounds contributes to the overcoming of shame and despair, freeing people to face their troubles and to take advantage of opportunities for recovery.

"Writing poetry affords a way of expressing oneself so that others can understand. And having done that one is no longer a lonely voice—a small purple light going on and off in the snow that no one sees—as one patient put it.

"The act of writing a poem is different from the act of speaking, because the written word is felt by the writer and experienced by others as more earnest than spoken utterances. Perhaps this is because the written vord is permanent—it stands as something for which ne is responsible. Because it is there it cannot be lisavowed. Hence, one regards a written statement vith an element of awe with which the same statement, if uttered, would not be regarded. At the same ime, since the poem issues from the imagination, it provides a mask which is felt by the poet as protective, o that truth can be uttered in the poem that could not be articulated in discourse.

"The quotation at the head of the chapter is a good llustration of what I mean and how the process works. The patient who made the statement didn't—couldn't—*say* it to me. She wrote it on a piece of paper, vhich she handed to me.

"That incident will give you an indication of how ewarding this work is for me. I am privileged to be loing it."

Patients also write poetry in the VSA Creative Writng Project at Goldwater Hospital in New York City, vhich has been operated since 1985 in partnership vith PEN, American Center, which is the international association of professional writers. Goldwater is a city hospital and a long-term care and rehabilitation acility for people who are chronically ill and/or have physical impairments.

The poetry workshops often feature well-known guest poets like Sharon Olds, winner of the 1984 National Book Critics Award for poetry. The project coordinator says, "The poetry project has developed into a powerful tool for rehabilitation and spiritual growth or everyone involved."

A sample:

> *If I was Paul the King*
> *I'd want for nothing*
> *If I was Diamond Jim Brady*

On each arm I'd have a pretty lady.
If I was Rockefeller the millionaire
I'd spend it fast everywhere
If I was Steve Brody,
Off a bridge I'd dive
Just to escape this everyday jive.
If I was, Wait! A problem I see
If someone else I was to be
Then who would be me?

Poet-in-the-Schools
Jack Kreitzer

The man who was working intently with a poetry group at the Very Special Arts Festival at the Kennedy Center in Washington, D.C. broke away for a few minutes to talk to us. "Many, many, maybe most, people think poetry is too hard, that they could never try it,' he said. "But once they try it, they find that taking the risk has a certain dignity to it. That's what the arts do for handicapped people: they confer on people the opportunity to be something more than handicapped. The arts confer on anyone—everyone—the dignity of taking the risk to be human."

Mr. Kreitzer, of South Dakota, was going to be a doctor and studied medicine for five years. When he was half way through medical school, he left for poetry. Better to be a struggling writer who enjoys what he's doing, he thought, than a successful doctor who is miserable. He has two books published so far. As a poet he got mixed up with education and now is an educational consultant in South Dakota, working with handicapped people, normal people, gifted people. As an artist-in-the-schools, he works with pupils to teach them how to make poetry. He also works with parents

170

and teachers, trying to impart to them concepts that will help them understand poetic forms of expression.

During our conversation, Mr. Kreitzer told us, "We can no longer look just at the disabilities of those who are handicapped. We need to focus on their abilities. Poetry—all the arts—allow them to be more human, give them a channel to let out their ideas and feelings and not be trapped with that stuff inside them.

"I know people who are alive today who would not be if they didn't have poetry. I worked with several emotionally disturbed people who also have physical and other sorts of handicaps. Several were suicide candidates and had attempted it before. But once they found poetry they had a vehicle to let that same energy go in a positive way.

"We are, you know, more alike, much more alike, than we are different. Another thing that handicaps those of us who are called normal is our attitudinal barriers, which we use to fend off people whom we perceive as different from us. We are all handicapped to some degree. Suppose you wear glasses; well, glasses are visual crutches."

We wanted to hear about the poetry teaching Mr. Kreitzer is doing today in South Dakota, but he had to return to the group he was working with at the Festival. In an article he wrote for the magazine *Design*, he described his beginning as a maker of poetry with handicapped people and some of what he does today:

> It was one of those early April days in the Midwest when it's almost spring but not quite: gray, windy, scattered, cold. My confidence felt as though it were riding in tandem with the weather on our way to Augustana College in Sioux Falls. The fine arts building there would be lent for a day to house a Very Special

171

Arts Festival—a chance for artists of various disciplines (painters, calligraphers, musicians, actors, poets, dancers) and for physically or mentally handicapped people to create art together and so to celebrate life and teach one another.

Although I'd conducted several week-long residencies in poetry in schools across South Dakota at every level for over five years under the auspices of the South Dakota Arts Council, I had not been involved with special education classes. My apprehension came from not having tried techniques of "provoking" poetry with the handicapped as well as not having dealt with people who've been long segregated in institutions.

It didn't seem that poetry would lend itself to effective creative expression with the mentally handicapped; but the Very Special Arts Festival was a chance to do art for its own sake and for the self-discovery of unsuspected capabilities by the handicapped.

My confusion was resolved by relearning that handicapped people are human, too—that the same sparks I'd used with "normal" students apply here, the only modification being my taking dictation on pad, blackboard, or tape recording.

Actually, we are all handicapped in one way or another, if only attitudinally. In our preconceptions that mentally handicapped individuals can deal only in the concrete and are lost in the abstract, we handicap ourselves—and the handicapped people we deal with as well. Many of those in supposedly lower mental categories frequently wrote more startling, perceptive images and insights than I encountered in the peer-group-structured imaginations of regular classrooms. This I did not expect.

We composed poetic collaborations while other groups in the building acted, made music, painted, and danced. They were in part stimulated by using pieces of art like the painting of *The Man in the Red Hat*, by Rudolf Hauser, which was taken from the *Beatles Illustrated Lyrics* exemplifying "The Fool On the Hill." We also used comparisons and free associations with emotions, colors, days of the week, senses, mothers and whatever was available in the room. Even the ordinary and everyday have poetic qualities.

A Black Poem

Black is a crow
Black is a blackboard, a blackbird
it is all burned, it is a black road
it is a shoe, the pupil of an eye
telephone wires, a window frame
it is a cat
Black is a door to your dreams

From the Crippled Children's School came four bright boys and two shy girls who were unimpaired mentally but who were in wheelchairs or braces and crutches because of polio or birth defects. With musician Mike Connor we improvised a song that became at once incisive and reflective of life. The words became strikingly organic as their suggestions and editing honed it from a simple suggestion of dark into a complete trinity of art, poetry, and music. From not expecting enough, I was finding myself slapped by active imaginations—self-searching and cathartic in venting frustrations at their own situations.

The Dark

darkness is an empty closet
darkness is a piece of space
darkness is a silent night
darkness is a deep problem

nothing is dark for the girls
even though darkness is a gloom
it is blind, it is a long war
darkness is not being loved

hope is light it's like the sun
breaking through the cold dark night
warming up your earth once again
putting an end to the dark

The two groups of mildly mentally handicapped were the greatest surprise and satisfaction. From classes that I had expected to be plodding and basic came floods of spontaneous images that I could barely record at equal pace. Images of totally unexpected associations that made beautiful metaphors, fantasy unmuffled by social acceptance, imaginations without restraints, innocent sensitivity, enduring senses of humor. Several times incisive, powerful similes and perceptive insights into the society that has dominated and controlled or belittled them surfaced in their poems. Just as often their sharp gaze saw themselves as the mournful, green-faced *Man in the Red Hat.*

CHAPTER NINE

Prose
Words That Can Help

We speak of therapy as art
rather than science
because there are many beliefs and approaches,
and because the human feeling that goes into therapy
is as important as the methods.

—DISABLED VILLAGE CHILDREN

One of the most widely read authors in the world today is a disabled writer/artist who devotes his words and pictures to aiding millions of people around the world who are handicapped by physical or mental limitations, disease, poverty or lack of education. He also encourages others to reproduce and distribute his work without payment of royalties to him.

Where There Is No Doctor

He is David Werner, 53, of Palo Alto, California. His first major book, *Where There Is No Doctor*, was published in 1977 and there are in print today a good deal more than two million copies in more than 40 languages, including pidgin English. It's a training manual for health workers in rural areas of poor countries where physicians are not available. In use in 150 countries, it is the world's most widely used primary health-care manual for community health workers. Along with his other major health books, the manual assures Mr. Werner a place as one of history's greatest health educators.

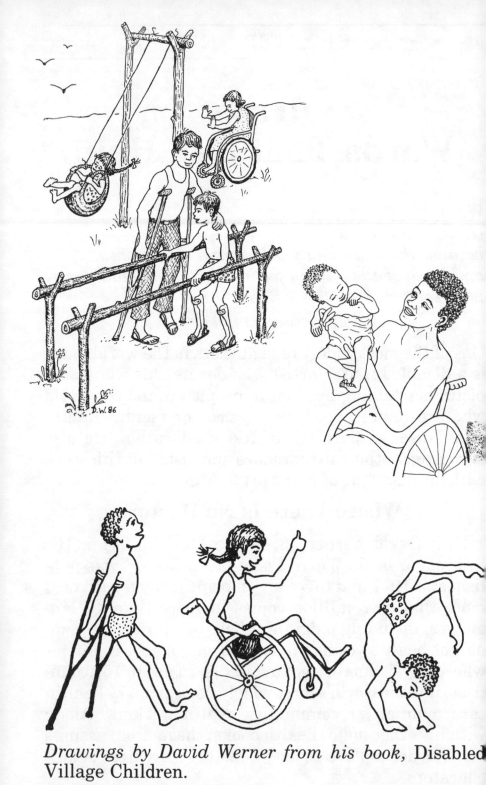

Drawings by David Werner from his book, Disabled Village Children.

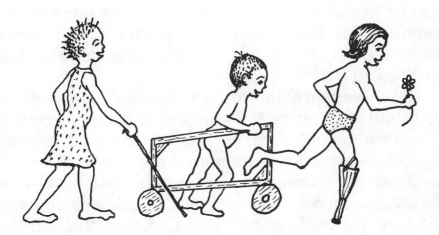

Intended for people of limited general education and reading ability and little or no experience in the health field, the manual is a marvel of simplicity and clarity in the presentation of its often ingenious solutions to health problems in areas where both trained professionals and money are in short supply. The volume is profusely illustrated with Mr. Werner's line drawings. Many governments have used it as a model for creating their own health training materials.

In a review, David Morley of Britain's Child Health Institute, who also is an internationally recognized writer on health, said this: "From time to time an outstanding book is produced which meets an immediately felt need. Such is David Werner's book, *Where There Is No Doctor*, which to me is the most important book to have come out in the health field in the last ten years."

Helping Health Workers Learn

In 1982 there came *Helping Health Workers Learn*, a book of methods, ideas and aids for instructors at the village level. And in 1987 Mr.Werner published *Disabled Village Children,* which is a 670-page manual for health workers, rehabilitation workers and the families of children who have impairments. Both seem certain to have a publication history much like that of *Where There Is No Doctor.*

Of the book on children, Sarah Cook of International Disability Education & Awareness in Britain declared: "It's brilliant. Working out the content of our course, and of each session, we realized just how much work and careful thinking has gone into that book, condensing the most important bits in each topic. I really like the political commitment that runs through the pages, too."

An excerpt from Mr. Werner's introduction to the

manual on disabled children illustrates his style and his philosophy. His approach to rehabilitation work with children who have impairments will be of interest to every disabled person because, with Mr. Werner's book on the way to reaching every corner of our country and undoubtedly many other countries, his views are likely to become widespread.

Disabled Village Children

This book was written from the "bottom up," working closely with disabled persons and their families. We believe that those with the most personal experience of disability can and should become leaders in resolving the needs of the disabled. In fact, the main author of this book and many of its contributors happen to be disabled. We are neither proud nor ashamed of this. But we do realize that in some ways our disabilities contribute to our abilities and strengths.

In many rehabilitation manuals, disabled persons are treated as objects to be worked upon, to be "normalized" or made as normal as possible. As disabled persons, we object to attempts by the experts to fit us into the mold of normal. Too often "normal" behavior in our society is selfish greedy, narrow-minded, prejudiced—and cruel to those who are weaker or different from others. We live in a world where too often it is "normal" and acceptable for the rich to live at the expense of the poor, and for health professionals to earn many times the wages of those who produce their food but cannot afford their services. We live on a wealthy planet where most children do not get enough to eat, where half the people have never seen a trained health worker, and where poverty is a major cause of disability and early death. And yet the world's leaders spend 50 billion dollars every three weeks on the instruments of war—an amount that could provide primary health care to everyone on earth for an entire year!

Instead of being "normalized" into such an unkind,

unfair, and unreasonable social structure, we disabled persons would do better to join together with all who are treated unfairly, in order to work for a new social order that is kinder, more just, and more sane.

This large book, then, is a small tool in the struggle not only for the liberation of the disabled, but for their solidarity in the larger effort to create a world where more value is placed on being human than on being "normal"—a world where war and poverty and despair no longer disable the children of today, who are the leaders of tomorrow. [emphasis in original]

Top-down rehabilitation manuals too often only give orders telling the "local trainer," family member, and disabled person exactly what they "must do." We feel that this is a limiting rather than liberating approach. It encourages people to obediently fit the child into a standard "rehabilitation plan," instead of creating a plan that fits and frees the child. Again and again we see exercises, lessons, braces, and aids incorrectly, painfully and often harmfully applied. This is done both by community rehabilitation workers and by professionals, because they have been taught to follow standard instructions or pre- packaged solutions rather than to respond in a flexible and creative way to the needs of the whole child.

In this book we try *not* to tell anyone what they *must* do. Instead we provide information, explanations, suggestions, examples, and ideas. We encourage an imaginative, adventurous, thoughtful, and even playful approach. After all, each disabled child is different and will be helped most by approaches and activities that are lovingly adapted to her specific abilities and needs.

As much as we can, we try to *explain basic principles* and *give reasons for doing things*. After village rehabilitation workers and parents understand the basic principles behind different rehabilitation activities, exercises, or aids, they can begin to make adaptations. They can make better use of local resources and of the unique opportunities that exist in their own rural area. In this way many rehabilitation aids, exercises, and activities can be made or done in ways that *integrate rather than separate* the child from the day-to-day life in the community. . . .

A note about the feminine pronoun used in the excerpt: In an effort to be even-handed, Mr. Werner explains, he avoids the awkward he/she approach, by using pronouns of both genders interchangeably throughout the book.

Mr. Werner has Charcot-Marie-Tooth syndrome, which causes a progressive atrophying of muscles. Although it affects his legs, he does not need a wheelchair or crutches. The condition has caused him to lose fine motor control in his hands and he has to make the drawings for his books larger than needed and then have them reduced.

When we asked him about the motive that drives his intense involvement with and on behalf of the world's poorest, least educated and most powerless people, he responded: "I have always had strong sympathy and empathy for the underdog and I think my being disabled contributed to that. For an American to have a condition while growing up that marginalizes him, that leads others to make fun of him for being different, gives him a certain understanding, a certain perspective about prejudice. It gives him a different way of looking at the world. It could have made me angry at the world, but it didn't. Of course, there are times when I do get angry. I get very angry when I see anybody mistreated or abused for being different or for being weaker than other people."

Mr. Werner's books are direct outgrowths of a decades-long involvement he has had with health programs for villagers in the mountains of Western Mexico. "I was a biology teacher in a high school and in 1964 I spent a vacation in the Sierra Madre, studying and drawing bird and plant life," he recalls. "I was struck by the warmth and friendliness of the people. And I was also struck, quite forcefully, by the enormity of their health problems. When I returned to school I picked the brains of some people who had experience in tropical medicine, then got a group of students to help me put together some simple first-aid and medical kits. We included with the text some easy-to-follow Spanish-language instructions. For those who couldn't read at all, we made comic-book-like illustrations and color- coded different medicines so they could still follow the directions. We delivered the kits ourselves and we spent about a month in the area. That trip convinced me that more help was needed and I decided to spend about a year there, taking a leave of absence from my job.

"To raise money to support myself and my work for the people I made a series of paintings for sale. They were of birds and plants of the area in a style similar to Audubon's, but using a black-and-white brushing technique I had learned in Japan. Before I began teaching I went to the Orient to study religious philosophy. It was a sort of quest. I majored in zoology and ecology in Australia and then did a year of graduate study in English poetry and theatre at the University of Cincinnati in 1956 and 1957. After that I spent quite a while in India, six months studying Eastern philosophy, walking with Vinoba Bhave, Gandhi's successor in the land-reform movement, and studying educational alternatives.

"From India I went on to Japan, where I ended up studying with a Zen artist. One of the main things I learned from him was his admonition, 'If you look into the mirror and see your face, look deeper and see yourself, the brush comes after.' It was a wonderful experience. It lasted about three weeks and that's the only sort of semi-formal training I've had in art. But my father, a lawyer, also was a painter and I guess I picked up my love for drawing from him, which I had from quite an early age."

Project Piaxtla

During that first year in Mexico, Mr. Werner founded a primary health-care network in and around the village of Ajoya in the Sinaloa area of the Sierra Madre mountains. Known as Project Piaxtla, it is staffed and managed by villagers; Mr. Werner remains the director. The concept that lay people can and should be responsible for their own health care is a rock-solid principle with him and permeates all his work. In his first book he explained some of the concepts that underlie the principle:

> Ordinary people provided with clear, simple information can prevent and treat most common health problems in their own homes—earlier, cheaper, and often better than doctors.
>
> People with little formal education can be trusted as much as those with a lot. And they are just as smart.
>
> Basic health care should not be delivered, but encouraged.

Almost from the day the Piaxtla opened, parents brought disabled children and asked for help. But little was available, and that in far-away Mexico City. So Mr. Werner arranged with the Shriner's hospital in San Francisco to supply children with free surgery and prostheses. He and volunteers drove as many as 16 children at a time to San Francisco. When the children returned to the mountains considerably improved, some able to walk for the first time, the reputation of the clinic spread, and many more children appeared. Not all of them needed hospital care. Some needed only therapeutic exercise programs or prostheses to give them mobility.

The villagers' solution was to add a local, do-it-yourself formal rehabilitation program to their clinic. Local craftsmen converted an unused, mud-brick building into a rehab center. Able-bodied and disabled children helped build a playground using techniques and equipment that allowed both groups to use it. Housewives volunteered to provide room and board for visiting children and their families. From these beginnings grew *Disabled Village Children*, designed to help the estimated 50 million disabled children throughout the third world.

Mr. Werner's international standing is such that governments and nongovernmental organizations from around the world invite him to spread his health views, share his expertise and give advice to those who want to copy his work. He has been a consultant to the Pan American Health Organization, the Peace Corps, UNICEF, the World Health Organization and other health organizations as well as the governments of Mexico, Mozambique, Zimbabwe and the Philippines. In 1985 the World Health Organization awarded his Hesperian Foundation group of workers its first international award for Education in Primary Health Care. He has other awards and honors for his writing and for his work.

Hesperian Foundation

Despite his international stature and the kudos that has been heaped upon him and the little band of people who work with him in the Hesperian Foundation, their administrative organization and funding conduit, they remain determinedly simple in their attitudes toward their work and themselves. Their personal incomes and professional budgets both are nickel-and-dime affairs. To make the books they publish as available to as many people as possible, they keep the prices as low as possible. And they allow others to reprint their work at no cost provided the reprints are not sold at a profit. Consequently, the monetary returns from what they produce are miniscule compared to what they could be.

The humility that runs through the personal lives and professional work of Mr. Werner and his band of a dozen or so large-souled associates is perhaps best illustrated by the name of their foundation. Though the term Hesperian comes originally from Greek mythology, the situation it refers to bears no relation to what the foundation does. They took the name simply because it was convenient and time-saving to adopt. It was the name of a California street.

When we asked about the name we were told, "Only our work matters, not what we're called."

Essayist
Nancy Mairs

Of all the writers of English prose who explicate the disabled condition, the best is Nancy Mairs of Arizona. In her 1986 book of essays *Plaintext*, about half are devoted to exploring the meaning—to her, to her family and friends, and for those beyond her immediate ken—of her increasing disabilities and decreasing physical world. Her observations about this world are not intended to be inspirational, neither are they maudlin. Her writing is clear-eyed, hard-edged, astringent, provocative, sometimes brutal and quite often funnny. She has much to say to everyone, disabled or not. Consider this clear vision of her physical condition and of the language she uses so well:

> First, the matter of semantics. I am a cripple. I choose this word to name me. I choose from among several possibilities, the most common of which are

"handicapped" and "disabled." I made the choice a number of years ago, without thinking, unaware of my motives for doing so. Even now, I'm not sure what those motives are, but I recognize that they are complex and not entirely flattering. People—crippled or not—wince at the word "cripple," as they do not at "handicapped" or "disabled." Perhaps I want them to wince. I wanted them to see me as a tough customer, one to whom the fates/gods/viruses have not been kind, but who can face the brutal truth of her existence squarely. As a cripple, I swagger.

But to be fair to myself, a certain amount of honesty underlies my choice. "Cripple" seems to me a clean word, straightforward and precise. It has an honorable history, having made its first appearance in the Lindisfarne Gospel in the tenth century. As a lover of words, I like the accuracy with which it describes my condition: I have lost the full use of my limbs. "Disabled," by contrast, suggests any incapacity, physical or mental. And I certainly don't like "handicapped," which implies that I have deliberately been put at a disadvantage, by whom I can't imagine (my God is not a Handicapper General), in order to equalize chances in the great race of life. These words seem to me to be moving away from my condition, to be widening the gap between word and reality. Most remote is the recently coined euphemism "differently abled," which partakes of the same semantic hopefulness that transformed countries from "undeveloped" to "underdeveloped," then to "less developed," and finally to "developing" nations. People have continued to starve in those countries during the shift. Some realities do not obey the dictates of language.

Mine is one of them. Whatever you call me, I remain crippled. But I don't care what you call me, so long as it isn't "differently abled," which strikes me as pure verbal garbage designed, by its ability to describe anyone, to describe no one. I subscribe to George Orwell's thesis that "the slovenliness of our language makes it easier for us to have foolish thoughts." And I refuse to participate in the degeneration of the language to the extent that I deny that I have lost anything in the course of this calamitous disease; I refuse to pretend that the only differences between you and me are the various ordinary ones that distinguish any one person from another. But call me "disabled" or "handicapped" if you like. I have long since grown accustomed to them; and if they are vague, at least they hint at the truth. Moreover, I use them myself. Society is no readier to accept crippledness than to accept death, war, sex, sweat, or wrinkles. I would never refer to another person as a cripple. It is the word I use to name only myself.

The facts of Ms. Mairs life are these: She is 44. She was born in California, but grew up in New England. She took her bachelor's degree in English literature at Wheaton College in Massachusetts. From 1966 to 1972 she worked as a technical editor at the Smithsonian Astrophysical Observatory, the MIT Press, and the Harvard Law School. In 1972 she moved to Tucson, Arizona, and taught high school and college composition courses while studying for a Master's degree in poetry. She received a Ph.D. in English literature in 1984 and the same year won a major poetry award. Her book *In All the Rooms of the Yellow House* received first prize for poetry in the Western States Book Awards competition. She is married, has two children of her own and a foster son, and has grandchildren.

The truths of her life are these: In addition to multiple sclerosis, she has recurring attacks of agoraphobia, a fear of open spaces which prevents her from leaving her home. She also has bouts of depression which have led to several serious attempts at suicide. She was committed to a state mental hospital for a lengthy stay, during which she had electroshock treatments. Outside her wheelchair these days she can take only a few steps if aided by braces and canes.

Although all of Ms. Mairs's essays are strongly au-

tobiographical, not all of them are about her disabil
ities. Her acerbic and often self- deprecating wit shows
in all her writing, even when the subject concerns
the—we were about to say *happier*, but perhaps the
more accurate term is *easier*—times before the MS
made itself manifest. This poem catches the flavor
well:

> *The man who doesn't love me*
> *I love twice*
> *Once for his beauty*
> *Again for his sound sense*

With her extraordinary ability to capture the nu
ances of the human condition, Ms. Mairs is an impor
tant guidepost at the intersection of art and disability
In the world of letters without regard to the presence
or absence of bodily disabilities, she seems to us a
worthy successor to E.B. White, who for a couple o
decades at least was more or less our national essayist
the acknowledged master of the form. Ms. Mairs has
a similar ability to examine the minutiae of life in and
around herself and her household and to extract from
them meaning and significance for everyone. Highly
recommended.

KALEIDOSCOPE

Since it was born in 1980 the most important part o
the magazine *KALEIDOSCOPE* has not been its title
but its subtitle. In the beginning the subtitle was *Na
tional Literary/Art Magazine For The Disabled.* Sev
eral years later that was changed to *The Internationa
Literary & Fine Art Magazine by Persons With Disa
bilities.* In 1986 the subtitle became *Internationa
Magazine of Literature, Fine Arts, and Disability.* Fa
from being mere administrative fly-specking, the
changes are important because they reflect accurately

the publication's search for a niche in the arts scene, an attitude and a personality. This most recent subtitle is evidence that the publication has found all three.

The magazine's early confusion about its identity echoes the confusion that appears rampant in the community of serious artists (as distinct from hobbyists) who are disabled. Should they have their own artistic publications and art shows in which they are viewed as disabled artists, thus being segregated from the arts mainstream and consigned to what amounts to a disability ghetto? Or should they seek to function in the mainstream as, first, artists who, second, happen to be disabled? The evolution of *KALEIDOSCOPE* to its present stance on this issue may indicate that the latter view is gaining ascendancy. If so, the magazine's new ambience could properly serve as a guidepost to those organizations and nondisabled people who are concerned about events and directions where the arts and disability intersect.

The change in *KALEIDOSCOPE* is the work of a new editor, Darshan C. Perusek, who produced the twelfth issue, dated Winter 1986. In her editor's comment in that issue she explained her view of *KALEIDOSCOPE's* place in the world and how readers should regard those changes in subtitles:

> . . .The changes, including the last and, we hope, final one, are not seen as a reflection of editorial capriciousness; they are, in fact, a consequence of a continuing and intense discussion and debate among ourselves about what *KALEIDOSCOPE* is, what it ought to be, and how it can best serve the artists who *contribute* their work to it and the readers who read it. The question about what *KALEIDOSCOPE* is and what it ought to be was relatively easy to answer: it is and will continue to be a forum for disability-related

art and literature. What we have been debating so long is, "What exactly is disability-related art and literature?" Do we, for instance, define it by subject? If so, not only do we limit our artists and writers to write about nothing but disability but, even more dangerous, we tell our readers that the vision of disabled writers and artists, unlike that of their counterparts in the able-bodied world, excludes every aspect of the world they live in except one—their disability. A dangerous message, because it diminishes both the artist and his art. It says the disabled artist creates "disabled art," in the sense of limited art. But if the consequences of defining disability-related art by subject are dangerous, those of defining it by author (art by a person with a disability) are absurd, if not bizarre. Do we, for example, ask our contributors for medical records to establish bonafide disability? And how much disability really "qualified" as disability? Cane? Crutches? Wheelchair? (shades of that awful TV show "Queen For The Day"—the one who tells the most Job-like story wins the day, tiara and all). And what's the message here? Inspirational, of course. The same message as in so much popular and traditional "high-brow" literature—"Look what they can do!" A Victorian circus-show.

And so we changed the subtitle. We hope that the change is seen as more than an exercise in punctuation and clever word-juggling. It is, in truth, the result of our deeply-felt commitment to a certain view of art, which is that the artist must be free to create his vision, and the reader must, in turn, be freed by that vision— freed, that is, from the disabling consequences of thinking in stereotypical ways.

We know that, having said this, we have to ask ourselves in what way we can continue to keep the identity of *KALEIDOSCOPE* as a magazine of disability related art. The only answer here is that we will have to trust the judgment of our contributors and our own editorial discretion. We call this "calculated ambivalence."

"Calculated ambivalence" is a concept many will find useful beyond the confines of a magazine's pages. Editor Perusek and her staff will of necessity use it often to carry out their mission. While the editor quite correctly keeps her eye on the imprecise and enigmatic nature of "disability-related," in their public statements about the magazine, its parent, the Cerebral Palsy organization, has made a brave attempt to clarify the matter:

> The term "disability-related" needs explanation: As originally conceived, it meant art and literature by disabled artists and writers. However, the editorial policy of the magazine has changed to reflect a shift in emphasis and direction. The emphasis now is not on the disability of the contributors ("look what 'they' can do!") but on the experience of disability itself: what does the writer/artist say about it? How does it impinge upon his/her work? How does it illuminate the creative process? What does it say about the creative imagination? Second, the magazine has been opened to non- disabled writers/artists, thereby bringing in outsiders' perspectives on the issue and also broadening the readership. Third, the material published will be carefully reviewed and selected primarily for literary and artistic excellence, with the objective of maintaining a high standard.

In a note addressed to potential contributors the magazine says, "We are a serious, fine-art and literary magazine, which challenges readers to confront feelings about disability. We select material which projects valid roles, and hope to establish a substantive body of work in the field of disabled studies." In the current issue are such items as these:

Monet's Cataracts. James Ravin, M.D., an opthalmologist with an interest in artists and the arts, discusses the effects of the painter's visual impairment on his later art.

191

Literature, Medicine, and The Magic Lie. Lawrence Schneiderman, a physician who is also a novelist, a playwright and a writer of short stories, on the relationships between art, medicine, miracles and lies.

Distant Voices: The Personal Experience of Disability in the Soviet Union. Ethel and Stephen Dunn, specialists in daily life in the Soviet Union, discuss similarities in outlook between disabled people in the U.S. and the USSR. Both the Dunns have cerebral palsy.

There also is poetry, fiction, and an essay on the work of a photographer and more, most of which has little or nothing to do with disabilities. *KALEIDO-SCOPE* is published twice a year, in January and July.

The Disability Rag

It would not be seemly to leave a discussion of writing and disability without including *The Disability Rag.* There are those, of course, who may object that it isn't an artistic publication. "Not by a long shot!" we can hear some readers bellowing. But we believe that for this unique little publication it would be worth searching around for a category that would apply with which we could lift the edge of the artistic tent just enough for it to slip in.

The magazine has been called combative, strident, accusatory, confrontational, always ready to vilify, disparage, or give the back of its hand to the works of others. It also has been called honest, smart, sensitive, forward-looking, intelligent and with a clear vision. In our view, the little magazine is all of these and usually an awfully good read besides. It doesn't hesitate to take on even those who believe they are supporting and helping disabled people. Telethons to raise money for the disabled, for instance: "Why isn't the space program—or Star Wars defense research—paid for by a national telethon?" The magazine is not grateful for the fundraising efforts of Danny Thomas for leukemia and Jerry Lewis for muscular dystrophy, viewing the efforts as mawkishly sentimental and patronizing.

The *Rag* also has taken out after Richard Simmons, the TV exercise guru, who came up with a book titled *Reach for Fitness: A Special Book of Exercises for the Physically Challenged*. Seems innocuous, doesn't it? Not to the magazine: "His whole approach tends to sanctify the concept that disabled people have to 'overcome' and they're very 'special.' It's real sappy, and also misguided and superficial. He's gotten on this bandwagon—help the gimps and be trendy at the same time."

The magazine runs no ads, carries no medical stories and does not deal in profiles of heroes who are handicapped. It has a section titled *We Wish We Wouldn't See* in which it skewers what it feels are offensive portrayals of the disabled. In this section it rapped a TV special on "The Bravest Athletes in the World," meaning athletes with disabilities. It believes the lionizing of those it calls "supercrips" obscures the real needs of the majority of disabled people. The publication gets upset over such phrases as "*confined* to a wheelchair" and a "*victim* of leukemia," which it sees as making disabled people a pitiable and helpless underclass.

Much of the material in the *Rag* bears a message of disability-pride, similar in intent to the civil rights movement "black-is-beautiful" message. The magazine has suggested that readers call themselves "survivors" rather than "disabled," because in its view the former term carries more self-pride. Publisher Cass Irvin explains self-pride as an effort to reverse chronic self-contempt. In an editorial Ms. Irvin once wrote:

"Too many disabled people don't like disabled people. Too many of us don't believe we are a worthy cause."

Founded in 1979 by Mary Johnson, who is ablebodied, and Ms. Irvin, who is a quadriplegic, the magazine is a bimonthly, the approximate size of the weekly news magazines and is produced on newsprint rather than glossy paper. It has grown from an initial 40 subscribers to more than 5,000 around the nation. Its readership and its influence are far greater than the circulation would indicate. It has become so well known and so well thought of that it is quoted in *The New York Times*, *The Washington Post*, *Atlantic* magazine and similar mainstream publications. The *Rag*'s headquarters are in the homes of Ms. Johnson and Ms. Irvin in Louisville, Ky.

Once asked to analyze the *Rag*'s popularity and its impudent approach, was Kathy Williams, who, as President of Kentucky's National Rehabilitation Administration Association, is both closely familiar with the magazine and a member of the disability establishment. She declared: *"The Disability Rag* is outrageous! This publication espouses the heretical belief that persons with disabilities should have control over their own lives. The *Rag* discusses independent living, attendant care, attitudes, accessibility, telethons, transportation, medical care, vocational rehabilitation, and the list is endless. The *Rag* believes in people with disability causing social change and attitudinal change. The *Rag* is a forum for views of persons with disabilities, and, at once, the *Rag* is classy, tacky, ethical, unprincipled, naive and wise. I do not always agree with the *Rag*, but what a fresh approach—a publication that states that all is not great and that change can happen and that the change can be caused by the people affected."

Another epithet that applies to the *Rag* is "paradoxical." It views itself as the only periodical that deals with disability as a civil rights issue. As such, it is hugely popular in the disabled community—despite the fact that it sometimes makes a target of the disabled themselves. In the May/June 1987 issue, for instance, the lead article is titled *Backlash!*. When reading the following excerpt keep in mind that most of its power and bite come from the fact that the *Rag* is a national leader and important national voice in championing the cause of civil rights for disabled people.

All is not well with our Movement. In our struggle for dignified, meaningful lives, we've alienated able-bodied people, on whom we depend for our daily, if not hourly, needs.

How have we alienated them?

Our movement philosophy proclaims that we, disabled people, just like other minorities (blacks, women, native Americans) are oppressed by the people who hold power over us—in our case the nondisabled people. What causes our suffering, runs this philosophy, is not our disabilities in and of themselves, but a society which, out of pure hatred, has systematically excluded us and relegated us to the status of non-humans. If only we stick together and fight until nondisabled society removes the barriers it's erected against us, everything will be paradise.

We model our struggle on that of the black civil rights movement, with its fight for self-affirmation, and its anger against the ways of whites. . .

Disabled people, however, are in a different position. Nature, not an unjust social order, has made us dependent upon ablebodied people—and that will always be the case.

Suppose all our demands were suddenly met? A job for every disabled person; every building and all transportation accessible, unlimited, free attendant care. A disabled person would still need a nondisabled person to get out of bed in the morning.

Anger has always been a part of the experience of being disabled. The anger disabled people feel is a uniquely frustrating anger that, like shouting at the rain to go away, accomplishes nothing. The anger is agonizing and never-ending.

There is much seductive comfort in the thought that if we scream and kick at society long enough, society will take away all our pain.

We adopt the rhetoric of the oppressed, endlessly debating among ourselves whether to call ourselves "gimps" or "crips." We scrutinize our portrayal in the media. We come to believe we have less and less in common with our nondisabled associates, whom we reject as leaders, advisors and role models, no matter how wise or imaginative they may be. In this way we avoid confronting the brutal reality: Our disabilities are forever, and no social revolution is going to zap us out of our wheelchairs.

Anger begets anger. The anger of our movement is aimed at ablebodied society. "You have kept us down," it says. "You are responsible for our second-class citizenship." Our movement is systematically rebuking and bludgeoning nondisabled people.

And nondisabled people are angry about it. The exasperated personal-care attendant feels exploited. Nondisabled drivers resent the favored parking spaces allowed disabled people at supermarkets. There's a substantial movement afoot to let disabled newborns die. Everywhere this anger is making itself apparent. . .

We in the movement often speak of "society" and "disabled people" as two separate entities. But we *are* society. We form opinions; we shape the attitudes of others. We are human beings first; disabled people second. If we keep this in mind, the necessary dialogue will become all the easier.

We cannot make it alone; and, if we could, our isolation would be excruciating. The hostile separatism we are pursuing has a fearful price. Let us direct our energies toward reconciliation and understanding, in the compassion common to all humanity.

Voice Indexing for the Blind

Coping with the written word, whether it is *Disability Rag*, or *KALEIDOSCOPE* or a great research library that is inaccessible to wheelchairs, has always been a problem for those who have visual or other disabilities. For those who are blind or have low vision, looking up specific items within a book is a particular burden.

There are high technology solutions for many students, rehab clients and adults who must do research tasks. But assistive devices, and even human readers, may not be available at the right time and place. Or the need may be to take notes or to look up something in last week's recorded notes. The user should be able to do this without asking for or waiting for someone else. In many of these situations, voice indexing may be the answer.

A sighted person looks up an item in a book, magazine or report by glancing at the chapter titles or the subject headings that are printed in distinctive type and set apart so as to be instantly recognized. When a blind person wants to look up something in a recorded cassette, there have, in the past, been no such descriptive guideposts. At best, the Library of Congress and other cassette-producing organizations flagged chapters with *beep* sounds on the tape. But to find something within a chapter has remained a time-consuming, hit-or-miss proposition. Although neither of the authors is visually impaired, we record most of our interviews on tape and for years have been acutely aware of how laborious and frustrating it can be to find a particular section within an hour-long tape.

But now comes voice-indexing. With this technique, you scan the tape at fast forward, which is about 16 times faster than normal speed. At each indexed section you will hear—in normal speed and tone—the index term. You switch the machine to normal speed and you will be within a few seconds of the indexed section. Although primarily developed for people who write and research, the technique is also useful for musicians who wish to record and locate particular sections of long works. It would be of great value to composers.

Special recorders or cassettes are not needed. Cassettes can be indexed and played back on many—though not all!—run-of-the-mill recorders. Voice-indexed cassettes can be played on certain models of 2-track or 4-track recorders; or on a special 4-track cassette player, such as those issued by the National Library Service for the Blind and Physically Handicapped, a division of the Library of Congress. The NLS machines are loaned without charge to blind and other print-handicapped persons through nearly 160 regional and subregional libraries for the blind.

The indexing does not require professional technicians. It can be done by family members, friends, classmates, or by a special education teacher who has just a few extra minutes to devote to a visually impaired student. People who have vision problems also can index tapes they make themselves.

The technique is quite new and is not widely known. It was developed by a retired librarian, James Chandler of College Park, Maryland. He retired in 1972 and the following year began working as a volunteer with low-vision, blind and other handicapped people. As a librarian, he had spent his life with the eternal research problem—how to find a small, but important, item in a large mass of material. "Braille was not a solution," he told us, "because only 10 percent of blind Americans can read Braille."

In addition to his long experience in libraries, Mr. Chandler had some inventive genes going for him. On display in the Smithsonian Institution in Washington, D.C., is a sewing machine for which his grandfather was granted a patent.

It took Mr. Chandler five years to perfect a solution that is simple, practical and highly effective—voice indexing on audio cassettes. Taking his new concept to government and nongovernmental agencies in search of funds to set up a voice-indexing operation, he met with stone walls. "Many government and agency people," he told us, "still really do not believe that blind and visually impaired people are capable of serious work." So, determined to forge ahead on his own, he set up a nonprofit organization, Voice Indexing for the Blind, Inc., to get out the word about voice indexing, to index useful works, to test recording machines and to distribute catalogues of available voice-indexed materials. For Mr. Chandler all of this is a labor of love.

Voice indexing can be done so easily and so cheaply and can be of such great help to anyone doing research, that we felt it would be a service to readers to show how it is done. Here are Mr. Chandler's instructions on how to go about it.

Procedure for Sequential Voice Indexing on a 2-Track or 4-Track Cassette Recorder

Purpose

• To produce a tape-recorded text, interspersed with index terms that are voice-indexed. Each index term precedes the text to which it applies.

Advantages of Procedure

• Recording and playback can be done on the same machine.

• A voice-indexed cassette made on a 2-track recorder can be played on track 1 or on a 4-track machine; a voice-indexed cassette made on track 1 or a 4- track recorder can be played on a 2-track machine.

• Some inexpensive general purpose cassette recorders can be used. (See Appendix)

• Very little instruction is required.

• Sequential voice indexing is especially useful for reference material which will be used chiefly for looking up specific passages.

Disadvantages

• On some machines, the signal quality of the index terms may only be from fair to good.

• If you are listening to a cassette that was prepared on a different machine, the index terms, running at Fast Forward, may sound faster or slower than a normal speaking voice.

• If one wishes to listen to the entire text without using the index feature, there will be annoying gaps in the text.

• Voice indexing drains battery power quite rapidly. Use an AC cord or the appropriate voltage adapter and plug into a wall outlet.

• This procedure does not provide for voice indexing a tape on which text has already been recorded.

Equipment

• A cassette recorder (2-track or 4-track) capable of recording at Fast Forward. On such machines the words "Cue" and "Review" are usually printed on the Fast Forward and Rewind buttons, respectively.

• Before a machine is purchased for this purpose, it should be tested by inserting a cassette; pressing the Record, Play and Fast Forward buttons simultaneously; and speaking a few words. Rewind a few seconds and then press the Play button and the Fast Forward button simultaneously. The words you have just spoken at Fast Forward should be heard in a normal voice.

Recording Procedure

1. Press Record and Play buttons simultaneously and record introductory matter at normal speed. Introductory matter should include:

> This recording is sequentially voice-indexed. The text and the index terms are on the same track, one after the other. The voice index feature can be used on cassette machines that have cue and review capability. To hear the index terms, press the Play button and the Fast Forward button simultaneously. When you hear the index term you want, stop the machine. Then press the Play button and listen to the text at normal speed.

2. Stop the machine.

3. To record an index term, press Record, Play and Fast Forward buttons simultaneously, wait one second to permit the machine to reach full Fast Forward speed, and say the index term in a normal speaking voice. All three buttons must remain down during the step; except that on the General Electric cassette recorder distributed by American Print House (APH/GE) it is not necessary to press the Play button.

4. Stop the machine.

> NOTE: If your recording machine puts a squeal on the tape when recording at Fast Forward, the squeal can be partially eliminated as follows:
> a. Rewind a few seconds.

b. Press Play and Fast Forward buttons simultaneously, stopping immediately after the end of the index term.

5. Press Record and Play buttons simultaneously; wait four or five seconds; and proceed with the recording of the next section of the text.

6. Stop the machine.

7. Repeat steps 3 through 6 as needed.

Listening Procedure

When you are listening at regular playback speed and reach the end of a section of text, the following recorded index term may produce a squeal for approximately half a minute. This can be avoided by pressing the Fast Forward button at the beginning of the squeal and holding it down until the end of the index term. If you are using a cassette player distributed by the National Library Service for the Blind and Physically Handicapped, you must stop the machine before pressing the Fast Forward button.

Searching for an Index Term

1. On a recorder other than the APH/GE:

a. Press the Play button and the Fast Forward button simultaneously to engage the "cue" feature. Hold both buttons down until you hear the index term you want.
b. When the index term is completed, stop the machine.
c. Press the Play button.
d. The text should be heard in a few seconds.

2. On the APH/GE cassette recorder or the 4-track cassette player distributed by the National Library Service for the Blind and Physically Handicapped:

a. Press the Fast Forward button until you hear the index term you want.
b. When the index term is completed, stop the machine.
c. Press the Play button.
d. The text should be heard in a few seconds.

202

CHAPTER TEN

Music
Magic Sounds

The disabled person should always try
to separate ability from disability.
That's the basic element of a proper attitude.
If your legs don't work,
it doesn't mean your brain isn't working.
So, you use your brain.

—*ITZHAK PERLMAN*

Of all the arts, for most of us music has both the greatest and most immediate emotional impress. Hard to measure scientifically, its effects, nevertheless can be seen. Kay Lindblade, State Director of the Very Special Arts program in Wisconsin, tells of an orthopedically impaired young boy who was so unhappy with himself and his surroundings that he spent many weeks weeping in the hall outside his special education classroom. It occurred to someone to put him into a music program. Today he is the biggest and happiest ham in The Singing Six, a group of physically impaired children who perform throughout Wisconsin.

Music is the most pervasive and most encompassing of the arts. Most Americans go weeks, months and years without exposure to dance, drama, poetry or the visual arts, but in this age of radio and television, it is a rare American who goes through a day without exposure to music. So it is astonishing that music, with its enormous power to affect people, was not put to work helping people with handicaps until after World

War II. Music as therapy has been around a long time—David and his harp in the Bible, for instance—but only on a scattered, hit or miss, individual basis. The systematic study and organized use of music to help people with impairments began only in the fifties to help speed the recovery of wounded soldiers in the wards of the veterans hospitals.

What music can do for both temporarily and permanently handicapped persons was explained recently by Dr. Arthur Harvey, co-chairman at the Center for Music and Medicine at the University of Louisville School of Medicine in Kentucky, which researches the use of music in the medical field, with emphasis on prevention and rehabilitation. Dr. Harvey conducted a series of workshops and seminars sponsored by the Very Special Arts program in Hawaii in 1986. His message was reported in the Hawaii program's newsletter.

"Music is a means of growth for the handicapped, to develop motor, perceptual, auditory and cognitive skills," Dr. Harvey told his listeners, many of whom were staff members working at facilities for people with disabilities. "Music nurtures language and social skills. It can also help those with disabilities to control or express their emotions, which is valuable when physical, mental or emotional difficulties block easy verbalization or the venting of built-up tension by means such as exercise."

The physician explained why our brains respond so quickly and so well to music. A major reason why all of us, even autistic and profoundly retarded persons react more easily and more emotionally is that music enters directly into the intuitive right hemisphere of our brains, bypassing the left side, which is devoted to dealing with verbalizing and reasoning processes ind is the side which in retardation may be more heavily damaged.

The first professional organization for people who use music to help others, the National Association for Music Therapy, dates only from 1950. A few years later a second organization, the American Association for Music Therapy, was set up. The profession is still small, with fewer than 4,000 practitioners across the nation,—so small that comparatively few Americans know it exists. Discussions with therapists make it clear that the possibilities music has for helping people with impairments are a very long way from being fully explored. The reason may be that its therapeutic capabilities are not understood by physicians generally and there has been slow acceptance by the medical community. Music is a subjective experience and what it accomplishes for a particular patient in a hospital or for a handicapped person usually is hard to measure in scientifically acceptable terms. Since it is the musical *process* that enhances learning, the therapists point out, growth and not achievement is the basic consideration. Research on the therapeutic effects is going forward, of course, but hard measurements of verifiable effects are not easy to come by.

Music Therapist
Ruthlee Adler

A trailblazer in the profession is Ruthlee Adler who now is the musical therapist at the Glenbrook Day School for exceptional children in Potomac, Maryland. She also has a private practice and is a widely known consultant and lecturer in her field. Majoring in music at the Music School of Indiana University in the early fifties, with a minor in psychology and experience in a mental hospital, Ms. Adler knew she wanted to be a therapist. But at that early date there were no music therapy courses at the school and she and a couple of other students pushed the institution into installing a course sequence which would permit them to earn degrees in Music Therapy.

In the other arts, rehabilitation is often a benefit, but seldom a direct goal. In music, however, the only goal is rehabilitation. No effort is expended to make someone a performer or to raise their musical skills beyond what is welcome as rehabilitation. In common with the other arts, however, music offers to those with physical or mental impairments which interfere with their ability to communicate a means of non-verbal expression. In the wards of the veterans hospitals it was found that music could reduce stress, relieve depression, relax people before and after surgery, reduce the need for medications and—sometimes—even relieve pain. The motions necessary to play an instrument also were found to help in physical rehabilitation. Hearing aids have been improved to the point where even people with severe hearing losses can make music.

Asked to explain music therapy, Ms. Adler says that there is such a wide variation of techniques and responses to them that explaining music therapy to a lay person is not simple. "The best way to put it, I guess," she essayed after a moment's thought, "is that I use music to reach somebody to bring them out on any level whatsoever. Music is calming, nonthreatening, and all-encompassing. It helps exceptional children to relax and focus their attention. While autistic and other disabled children may be indifferent to other kinds of stimulation, they do respond to music. We can use it as a learning tool to teach basic skills like numbers and language. And we can improve gross motor skills through marching and clapping to music and also the fine motor skills needed for playing an instrument.

"We can use music to teach all the different areas in development: motor communication, sensory integration, social interaction, cognition are all part of one's growth and development. If there is a deficit in one of those areas, I search for a way to use music to integrate and to energize an area which hasn't been energized before. Every child has a unique set of problems and I have to design a program to get at those problems, so it's rare that two programs would be exactly alike. I've even had to 'invent' some instruments."

This last was said with a laugh as she showed off a washtub "bass" she had cobbled together. "It's just a washtub. I drove a hole through the bottom and put a cord through it and tied it to a block of wood. Then I took a broom handle and cut a slit on the bottom so it fits on the bottom rim of the tub and tied the cord to the top. So now a child can see and feel the vibrations. Vibration is such an intangible thing, how do you teach a child that something vibrates and that's what sound is? With this, they can feel on their foot the vibrations coming through the bottom of the upside-down washtub and they can see and feel the cord moving. The tighter the broom handle, the higher the sound, which teaches them about high and low tones. The neat thing about it was that we sent it out for field testing and it came back with wonderful variations and adaptations for different handicapping conditions. Like if a child was visually handicapped and could see only red and yellow, they made the cord one of those colors and the broomstick the other one."

In addition to her work at the Glenbrook school, Ms. Adler in 1986 began working at the National Institutes of Health, the first music therapist to be invited to work with NIH patients. There she works with a variety of patient groups, ranging from children to geriatric patients who have Alzheimer's disease. For this latter group, and for people who have schizophrenia, she uses a technique for stress reduction that is common among music therapists. It is known as guided imagery and is used differently by different therapists, though the basic form is the same. This is how Ms. Adler uses it:

"My sessions last about an hour or so. First I set a scene for them, telling them, say, that they are going to visit a place that has special meaning for each one, a place where they feel relaxed and secure. I put on a music selection and they close their eyes while they listen to it and "visit" their special place. They have art materials and paper and they show where they went and what they saw, and we discuss it."

Another technique Ms. Adler and a few other therapists have begun using in recent years is to provide music and voice tapes for people who are in a coma as the result of severe injuries. It is known that people in a coma can hear and process information. The 20-year-old son of another Washington-area music therapist, Louise Lynch, in 1985 sustained severe head injuries in a car accident and was in a coma for seven-and-a-half weeks. Physicians warned his mother that if he survived, it was highly likely he would suffer mental impairment. His mother provided her son's nursing staff with anti-stress music tapes and tapes on which she talked about familiar events and the tapes were played by each nursing shift. Today her son is completely recovered and has suffered no perceptible brain damage. His mother is convinced that the daily tapes played a major role in his recovery.

"Louise Lynch's experience with her son convinced

me that there is a real need to provide tapes for people in a coma," Ms. Adler recalls. "I have made tapes for people who were in bad automobile accidents. And I urge family members to make tapes for comatose patients, especially if they can't visit the patient, because the person in the hospital needs to hear their voices. It can make a difference."

In 1982, supported by a grant from VSA, Ms Adler published a handbook for music therapists and special education teachers titled *Target on Music: Activities to Enhance Learning Through Music.*

Music schools now are beginning to learn that they have something special to offer on an organized basis to handicapped children. One such program is that of the Charleston Conservatory of Music, which is affiliated with the University of Charleston in West Virginia. A young and progressive organization, the Conservatory, which began only in 1979, has a number of outreach programs: a summer music camp, a music program for teachers, a touring chamber music ensemble and more. In 1981 they established a music program at the Edgewood Acres School for physically impaired pupils. All pre-school handicapped children in West Virginia's Kanawha County go to Edgewood Acres for assessment and therapy. Later some are mainstreamed into regular schools. Those who cannot be mainstreamed remain at Edgewood Acres.

The concept for the music program came from a Conservatory trustee, a Charleston businessman, the late Roy Pittman, who died in the spring of 1987. He told us of the benefits he saw the program bringing to the children and also of the needs that caused him to suggest it:

"In West Virginia, as in much of isolated Appalachia, we have children with a high incidence of birth defects. In Kanawha County alone, which is around

209

Charleston, we have almost a thousand handicapped children. These youngsters, faced with long-term physical impairments, need assistance to cope with their lives. We want to help them become whole persons through music. By working with them, we can open their eyes to a new understanding of their physical selves. We can help them learn what they can or cannot do. Often they discover they are not as limited as they first thought. The mouth that never closes does close enough to blow a brass instrument. The child who cannot speak grunts the rhythm to a song. The boy without the use of his hands can play a bugle. The cerebral palsy victim can sing. The fearful child finds new and uninhibited avenues of expression through music."

Music Therapist
Nadine Wobus

Nadine Wobus is a music therapist who also is a performer and also is physically impaired. Because of childhood polio her legs don't function. The disease prevented her hips from fully forming and they go out of joint and she has curvature of the spine. She uses leg braces, back braces and crutches. On occasions when she has to remain in one place for a long time she uses a wheelchair. Ms Wobus is a singer, a coloratura soprano with a three-octave range, who specializes in jazz. The 35-year-old therapist, who is petite, says that in addition to the therapeutic programs helping her patients they also help her:

"Because of the curvature of my spine I have reduced lung capacity and I get pneumonia and bronchitis a lot. But after people have heard me sing they ask, 'How do you get that big sound out of such a little body?' It's through the vocal exercises and the breathing ex-

Nadine Wobus is a music therapist. She is also a coloratura soprano with a three-octave range who specializes in jazz.

ercises. And when I do them with patients, they help me too."

When we asked how audiences react to her disability, Ms. Wobus responded:

"When they first see me they think disability, but when they hear me sing they forget the handicap. Except for the agents, the people who hire you. They can't get past the disability. Not for a female anyway. If I was a male they might. But the audiences get past it without trouble."

When she was studying music therapy at Hofstra College on Long Island, Ms Wobus performed around New York City at a number of clubs and halls that served as showcases for young performers. She explained for us what her performances were like:

"I always requested a high stool, which I made part of my persona. The steps up to the stages in the showcase places were very high and there were no railings. I overemphasized the struggle of getting up the stairs because people would think 'Oh, she'll never make it up those stairs!' So I would key into that. Then I would hoist myself up on the stool and they would think 'Is she going to fall?' Then I would put my crutches down and open my mouth and they would forget the whole thing. And they would love me because I'd built up the expectation in them that 'We'll love her anyway even if she can't sing.' Then when they heard me they were very pleased—'Oh, she can sing *too.*' It was all part of the persona.

"I do that in my therapy sessions as well. And it turns my disability into an asset. It works for me. It helps. You use whatever you've got."

Ms. Wobus described how music helped a young boy who was institutionalized in a state psychiatric hospital. Because he was awkward and fell a lot and had frequent seizures he had to wear a helmet. The other children made fun of him. He had a little garden plot he liked to work in and the other boys would periodically destroy it.

"He had a lot of emotion built up over all that," Ms Wobus recalled, "I had him make up his own songs and he went to the piano with me and made up a whole lot of songs, many of them with scary emotion in them. At Halloween we made up an entire instrumental drama and used percussion instruments to make scary sounds.

"How did this help him? His music experience carried over into his daily existence and made him feel better about himself. He thought, 'When I am at the piano I am not the klutz. I can make this wonderful music and it's mine and nobody can take it way from me the way they do with my garden.' The music gave him self-esteem—'Look what I can do.' There was no place else, no other situation, in that institution in which he could feel self esteem."

Another musician with a physical impairment who had experiences with booking agents similar to that of Ms. Wobus is world-renowned violinist Itzhak Perlman. He explains what happened when he was trying to begin his concert career:

Itzhak Perlman

"At first I had trouble getting a chance to play on the concert circuit. I couldn't understand why. I thought something was wrong with me musically. I thought everything was up to me, so I practiced harder. It simply never occurred to me that the difficulty was because I was disabled. Today, however, I believe that the booking agents thought to themselves, 'He's talented, all right, but he can't possibly travel. He's handicapped.' "

As he became established as a world-class musician,

the bane of Mr. Perlman's existence became the reviewers. He recalls that every review described him in the first paragraph as a disabled violinist who walked on crutches, as though it were odd for him to be able to play.

But after a while they forgot about the crutches," he remembers, "and I was very pleased. At last I had become first a good violinist and only second a man with a handicap. But now audiences, reviewers, everybody, is used to me. So I'd like them again to start saying I have a disability. I'd like to be a role model for the disabled." To further that purpose, he serves as a member of the Board of Directors of the Very Special Arts program.

A musical headliner for almost a quarter-century, Mr. Perlman in recent years has been making himself a spokesman for disabled people everywhere, most especially on the issue of the accessibility of public places. He recently declared:

"I've been in public buildings all over the world, so I know that the designers of them have no idea what it's like to use crutches or a wheelchair. One of the biggest architectural catastrophes ever is the new opera house in Sydney, Australia. It's a fantastic-looking place, with about a hundred steps to the front door— and no elevator. The audiences have to climb all those steps, and musicians have to haul their instruments up them. For the disabled the situation is hopeless.

"Oh I've played in halls that were well designed for access by people who are handicapped. But I've wised up about why that usually happens. Whenever I see ramps thoughtfully placed or an area well laid out for disabled people, I will ask, 'Who's disabled?' Usually it's an important local politician or a big financial supporter of the orchestra. Sensitive treatment for everyone should not have to be prompted by the bad experiences of important people. But for the moment, that's often the way it is."

When asked about his music and what, if anything, it does for him as a disabled person, Mr. Perlman responds:

"When you play the violin, you must hold it close to you. It becomes part of you. If you are mentally detached from your violin, your music will not be good. I am one with my violin. I enjoy playing. It is my ability."

Leon Fleisher

Another world-class musician while at the peak of his ability was suddenly hit by a disability that prevented him from performing. His world crashed around him and life lost all meaning. For two years he did nothing musical. Today, 20 years later, he is a respected conductor, a music director, an inspired teacher, and once again a soloist in demand. He is Leon Fleisher, who has long been acknowledged as one of the great pianists of his generation.

Now 58, Mr. Fleisher was the first American to win the famed Queen Elizabeth of Belgium International Competition in 1952. His recordings of the Beethoven, Brahms, Schumann, and Grieg concertos with George Szell and the Cleveland orchestra are regarded as definitive. He is also well known as a performer of chamber music with such groups as the Budapest and Juilliard String Quartets.

For more than a decade after winning the Belgian competition Mr. Fleisher was a productive performer who was kept extremely busy—too busy, it turned out—by the demands for performances and recordings. In the mid-sixties disaster struck. The famed pianist lost the use of his right hand for playing. The hand was not disabled in a general sense, it simply no longer could perform at the keyboard. What had happened was that the muscles and nerves controlling the fingers had been damaged—"through abuse from overwork," Mr. Fleisher says.

"What I did then was that I went into the deepest of depressions," Mr. Fleisher recalled in response to our query. "I was desperate. If you spend your life training to play and suddenly playing is no longer available to you, you believe your life has come to an end. The damage to my hand affected not only my public, playing life, but also my private life. The depression lasted about two years and I think it contributed to some extent to the termination of my second marriage. The only thing that kept me from jumping off the Chesapeake Bay Bridge is that I had to continue with my commitments for teaching."

World-famous pianist, conductor and teacher Leon Fleisher demonstrates a point to a pupil. Steve Wilcoxson

What brought him out of his despondency was an idea proposed by a couple of friends to start the Theatre Chamber Players of Kennedy Center, a chamber music group that would specialize in contemporary music. The key to getting Mr. Fleisher back into the mainstream of music was his friends' notion that he should direct the group. Mr. Fleisher took up the challenge, climbed out of his depression and has been director for the past 18 years.

Today Mr. Fleisher is busier musically than he was before his hand problem. He guest conducts for many of the world's great orchestras. He is professor of piano at the Peabody Conservatory in Baltimore, serves on the juries of many international music competitions, gives Master Classes at top music schools and festivals all over the country and is Artistic Director of the Tanglewood Music Festival. He also gives concerts with orchestras, playing music that has been written for the left hand.

The loss of his right hand for playing has changed his teaching techniques. He usually sits at the right side of his student and plays right-hand parts with his left hand. His ability at this technique is phenomenal and he makes no concessions, producing music as good or better than most musicians could do with their right hands. Other than his inability to play with it and some awkwardness in writing, the limitations of his hand and arm are not visible.

We asked if he was saddened that he could no longer play concerts as he used to.

"I'll tell you this," he declared in a spirited tone, "if it hadn't been for this injury to my right hand which prevents me from using it at the piano, as I did for most of my life, I would not have become the teacher that I am. I would not have become as aware of all the new directions in music. I would not have become a

217

conductor. I would not have helped start the Theatre Chamber Players at the Kennedy Center, and I probably wouldn't have wound up here at Tanglewood."

Ronnie Milsap

Country and Western singer Ronnie Milsap has been blind since birth. He has won three Grammys and has had at least 25 top hits. "You know," he says, "music is the way I've been able to break the handicap. Music has broken the barrier for me. Some people I know haven't been that lucky." He sang at VSA's 1984 festival at the Kennedy Center.

Mr. Milsap began his career with the guitar and later switched to the piano. When we asked him after his set at the Kennedy Center why he had made the change, the laugh with which he responded had just a slight touch of pique in it. "I'd put the guitar down on the stage and forget where it was and then I'd step on it. Busted more guitars that way. Ain't no way you can step on a piano and hurt it."

Stevie Wonder

Another blind musician is the peerless Stevie Wonder. Born blind, he spent his childhood in poverty in Detroit's black ghetto. His talent is so enormous that he had his first hit when he was 13, a jumping harmonica number titled *Fingertips Part Two*. Now 37, he has won more than a dozen Grammys and has had more than two dozen Top Ten hits. Of his ability to write hit songs he says simply, "it's the music that motivates me."

Ed Walker

Ed Walker, blind since birth, is not a musician but is very much in music. For more than 35 years he has been on the air, both radio and television, in the nation's capital. He began as a partner with Willard Scott, now the weatherman on the *Today* show. For 22 years they were the *Joy Boys* on radio, clowning around, ad libbing and performing an insane and wildly popular spoof of soap operas they called *As the Worm Turns*. Later he was co-host on a television talk show. But he is undoubtedly best-known for his years as a disc jockey on his own radio program *Play It Again, Ed*, which ran for five hours each Sunday.

At the Maryland School for the Blind near Baltimore they wanted him to become a piano tuner. Instead he enrolled in the School of Communications at American University in the nation's capital and went on to make history as probably the nation's only blind disc jockey. If he's not the only one, he's certainly the one with the longest on-air career record. In Washington his voice is legendary and in the fall of 1987 he was presented with the first Lifetime Achievement in Radio Award.

As a disc jockey, Mr. Walker builds his program exclusively out of the big bands that were popular in the thirties and forties, when he was growing up. The records come almost entirely from his own collection. A sighted friend helps him choose them. Mrs. Walker used to type his scripts in braille, but in recent years they have been done by computer.

Tony Mooney

Like the visual arts, music has its share of geniuses who in every other area of life and knowledge are developmentally retarded and whose abilities nobody can explain. One such is 11-year-old Tony Mooney of South Dakota. He performed his first recital on an electric organ at age five. At six he performed his first Country-Western nightclub act. Today his range is from all seven of Beethoven's Country Dances and Bach Minuets to *Rock Around the Clock*.

Tony was born three months prematurely and weighed about one pound. His eyelids were fused shut and he survived for months on high concentrations of oxygen.

A study done in Canada in 1958 found five blind-autistic children all born between the 24th and 28th week of pregnancy, all treated with high concentrations of oxygen—and all musically gifted.

Hope University

For people who have a great musical gift but who are otherwise mentally limited there is now a school in Anaheim, California, the only one in the nation and very likely the only one in the world. Founded in 1980 by Doris Walker, a Special Education teacher, it now has 40 students. Like many other felicitous discoveries, the genesis of Hope University was an accident. While teaching a Sperial Education class in a school in Buena Vista, California, during a music period she picked up a piece of sheet music and said out loud to herself, "I wonder what key we've been doing this song in?" An immediate response came from a blind, autistic student, Paul Kuehn, who had until then been considered untrainable. "The key of G," he told the teacher, loud and clear. Ms. Walker immediately began to train him to sing. Today he is a member of the school's singing group, the Hi Hopes, who have performed in, among other places, Las Vegas, Disneyland and the White House.

Through their instruction in music and art, the students at Hope University learn physical and emotional control. A number of them do so well that they are able to hold down part-time jobs. Ms. Walker explains: "We use music education, music therapy, drama, dance, performance and other arts to help our students to achieve new awareness, personal growth and change in their lives." She says she believes there should be dozens of schools like hers around the country.

The educational theory underlying the teaching methods of Hope University is known in school circles as the arts-infused curriculum. The theory basically holds that all other subjects such as reading, writing, history, anthropology, plus self-discipline and self-motivation, can best be learned through the medium of the arts. It does not mean merely adding an art room to the usual school nor just spending more time teaching art than is done at most schools. It means that art underlies every subject and infuses the teaching of them. Although it often meets stiff resistance from traditional educators, the arts-infused curriculum concept has in recent years slowly been making gains around the nation.

The Lab School

One of the best examples of the use of the arts-infused curriculum in the education of disabled people is The Lab School of Washington, D.C., which specializes in the education of learning-disabled children. Its Director, Sally Smith, who also is Chairman of the Learning Disabilities Program at American University, is widely recognized as an outstanding authority in the field of learning disabilities. When she searched for help for a severely learning-disabled son more than 20 years ago, she found a total lack of services in and around the nation's capital. Her response was to found The Lab School in 1967. In 1984 she added to the elementary and high school a night program for learning-disabled adults. At the request of the National Institute for Mental Health she wrote a book for lay-

Sally L. Smith, the Founder and Director of the Lab School, listens to one of her students, George Jeffries.

The Lab School

men on learning disabilities which has been reprinted many times.

The best way to give a reader who is unfamiliar with the subject an overview of what an art-infused curriculum is about is to quote a short section from Professor Smith's book: *No Easy Answers: The Learning-Disabled Child at Home and at School*:

> The arts have been a universal language among human beings since the world began. Gesture, movement, dance, rhythm, paintings, music, and masks carry symbolic meanings that often have no verbal equivalents; they are understood without words.
>
> It took the human race a long time to develop an oral language and far longer to evolve a way to write it down and read it. Children in their early years reenact the history of mankind. They understand gesture, rhythm, tone, and movement before they understand words. They sing and croon before they speak. They draw and paint before they form letters. They dance and leap and act out stories before they read. We need to make more use of this developmental sequence in our schools. Our elementary school children need to be immersed in the arts, which are considered essential to quality education. They foster intellectual, physical, social and emotional growth.
>
> Almost every child can be reached and taught innumerable skills through the arts. Yet rarely do schools take advantage of the rich and full education that can be derived from them. Schools tend to sideline the arts by relegating them to after-school activities or allowing drawing and music to be taught only once or twice a week. But some schools allow artistic activities to be scheduled in conjunction with a social studies or science project, or they employ the arts as preliminary training for eventual careers. In special education, the arts are sometimes treated as adjuncts to medical treatment, as therapy. The Lab School of Washington has pioneered in using the arts as vehicles to teach academic skills. . .

I developed a curriculum where half the day is spent in the classroom and half the day in the arts. Woodwork, all the arts and crafts, music, dance, drama, puppetry, and filmmaking offer pleasure and tangible results to children. Highly structured, clearly determined objectives have to be pursued through each art form. I programmed organizational skills, essential for approaching academic tasks, into the arts curriculum just as they had to be programmed into the classroom curriculum. If a child has not acquired the basic skills, he cannot learn to read even if he is taught reading several times a day. Reading readiness must be taught in the classroom, but it can also be taught successfully through the arts, and the two together form a more solid base.

Artists, art teachers, and art therapists can work on the same basic skills as a classroom teacher but in different and captivating ways. The same training in discrimination that is required for reading in the classroom is provided by discriminating one shape, sound, color, or direction from another in the arts. The skills for academic readiness are inherent in the arts: organizing and remembering sequences; assembling diverse elements into a meaningful whole; gauging relationships of size, shape, color, or volume; using and recognizing a symbol in varying contexts; and many more. With a prescription of precise objectives, the artist concentrates on the learning process while the child, doing what he enjoys, concentrates on the product he is creating.

There is a discipline underlying every artistic endeavor. People think of the arts as being very free; they are, but they become so only after one has mastered a set of basic skills. These skills must be taught in an organized, purposeful way. . .

While the arts-infused curriculum is an attractive and useful method of education for any child, it is particularly valuable for students with a wide range of disabilities.

CHAPTER ELEVEN

Very Special Arts
A Singular Concept

The Very Special Arts Program
makes it possible
for disabled Americans to participate
in the arts and enrich their lives
in the same way as all other Americans.
Through it, they can gain the opportunity
for self-expression within the context
of our rich cultural tradition.
This program deserves
the support and assistance
of all Americans.

      —RONALD REAGAN

Presidential Proclamation, May 1985

There were, of course, art programs for disabled people before VSA was invented, but they were scattered and isolated, some not as effective as they might have been, and liable always to sudden termination due to skittish funding, lack of understanding on the part of institutional administrators, departure of skilled teachers or other happenstances.

VSA's position on the arts-for-disabled-people scene today was summed up for us with refreshing succinctness by Gene Maillard, the organization's Chief Executive Officer:

"When VSA was founded, arts programs for people with disabilities already existed across the country.

What VSA did was to find those programs and provide the people already working in them—educators and artists—with a forum. This gave them an opportunity to show others what they were doing and to show the rest of the country what could be done. We brought these scattered efforts together into a unified program.

"From the people in the field we soon learned how great the need was. Educators, administrators and artists let us know what they were doing and how a national program like ours could help them reach more people. VSA's growth is one indication that there really was a tremendous need.

"It was largely through the initiatives and motivation of the people already in the field that VSA grew so rapidly. Without the support and enthusiasm of those people, the VSA program wouldn't exist, because the program relies on volunteers."

The stature VSA has achieved in its comparatively short life may be measured by the fact that during the 1984 Festival, which was held in Washington at the Kennedy Center, the participants, who had come from all over the nation, were invited to a reception at the White House, where they were greeted by Mrs. Reagan. The Congress also has designated VSA the national coordinating agency of arts programs for people with disabilities.

VSA founder Jean Kennedy Smith, whose sister Rosemary is mentally impaired, explained in a newspaper interview the genesis of the concept:

"With Rosemary, it was difficult for my parents to find many programs for mentally handicapped children. So I realized when she was growing up that this was a problem. It naturally interested me to see if there had been any development in this area. My sister Eunice has been very active with the Special Olympics for mentally handicapped children and when he was

226

a Senator, my brother John was active in getting legislation adopted.

"I was the chair of the Kennedy Center Education Committee in Washington. They were interested in arts education, and they felt the Kennedy Center could make a strong appeal in that direction. So I wondered what they did for children with handicaps. We conducted an investigation and found that things were being done throughout the country, but more or less in isolation. We felt we could get these groups to make an impact, and we could increase public awareness that these children could do anything, given the chance. So we formed a committee for that [National Committee for Arts for the Handicapped], and there's been a tremendously positive reaction."

Ms. Smith is on the VSA Executive Committee. She also is International Chairperson of the VSA Festivals program. She also works with other organizations that serve people with disabilities. She is a trustee for the Kennedy Center and has chaired its National Education Committee.

The value of her work with VSA has been commended by other civic groups. The New York chapter of the National Women's Division of the Albert Einstein College of Medicine of Yeshiva University has given her its *Spirit of Achievement* award, the Institute for Public Service gave Ms. Smith their Jefferson Award for Outstanding Public Service, the Council of Cerebral Palsy Auxiliaries in 1981 bestowed on her the Margaret Mead Humanitarian Award, and the People-to-People Committee for the Handicapped gave her their *Volunteer of the Year* award in 1979.

Ms. Smith's work with VSA follows her family's tradition. In addition to the work her sister Eunice does with the mentally retarded, her parents in 1946 set up the Kennedy Foundation, the only private foundation in the world that focuses exclusively on people with mental handicaps. And in addition to Rosemary, the family has a second member with a disability. He is Ms. Smith's nephew, Edward Kennedy, Jr., son of the Massachusetts senator. To arrest the spread of cancer, his left leg was amputated below the knee. He is a member of the board of VSA.

In 1986 the National Committee for Arts for the Handicapped was renamed Very Special Arts. Now in its 11th year, VSA is a resounding success. It has annual arts festivals in all 50 states, the District of Columbia and Puerto Rico as well as in some of the 40 countries which have adopted the VSA concept. The rate of growth has been phenomenal. In 1976 there were 27 festivals. By 1983 there were 250. And in 1987 there were more than 650. As the festivals have grown in number they also have grown in size. A single example: the first festival held at the Kennedy Center in Washington in 1974 was attended by 80 artists. A decade later, the 1984 festival at the Kennedy Center was attended by 750 disabled American artists. And from other countries came 166 artists, parents and observers.

The main purpose of the festivals is to demonstrate the power of the arts to develop self-expression, and release frustration in disabled people. They also are intended to show how the arts can increase general learning by individuals of all ages, indicating that art programs should be included in the general education of disabled people. Most of the art programs in each state go on throughout the year. The festival provides them with an annual platform, a forum and an audience to demonstrate what they have accomplished in the previous year.

VSA's Director of Program Operations, Eileen Cuskaden, described the festivals for us like this:

"The festivals are not only performances. There also are a lot of demonstrations and workshops for people like Special Education teachers who have been trained to use the arts, professional artists who have been trained to work with special needs people and who teach in schools under a grant from a state arts council, arts administrators. The festivals bring together lots of people who work in art, in education and in administration and funding. The workshops demonstrate to them what has been going on during the year and they can acquire both new knowledge and a quick overview.

"The festival is the one time when parents and general educators and special educators and arts educators are all together in a nonthreatening situation. They can talk to each other in a more informal, more leisurely manner than they usually do. They get to know each other, become friends and subsequently are better able to help their children and students."

When the VSA program began in the early Seventies, it was limited to youngsters of primary and secondary-school age. About 1981, however, it eliminated all age requirements. There is now neither an upper nor a lower age limit.

VSA's funding is a mixture of private and government money, with about 75 percent of the budget being contributed by the federal government's Department of Education. Many Americans believe that any activity supported by the federal government floats on a river of gold. That is not true for VSA. Its budget is around three million dollars a year, depending on the amounts contributed by corporate givers, with the federal contribution in the neighborhood of two million. By today's standards for governmental fiscal activity, such an amount is minute, a mere flyspeck. VSA, however, manages to stretch it quite far, getting a rather large bang for each buck. The VSA headquarters staff—they number about 30—estimate that their programs reach about one million persons each year. The money is spent largely through grants to each of VSA's statewide programs and for some special projects that are national in scope. The organization currently is making an effort to increase the financial support it receives from the private sector.

The national VSA budget is only part of the financial story. Each of its state organizations is incorporated as an independent private nonprofit organization and as such, each solicits its own contributions from businesses, foundations and individuals and when totaled up, these grants amount to far more than the three-million-dollar headquarters budget. So, while the VSA program is conceived and administered as a national program, the bulk of the financial support for its local programs is strictly a local matter. Private contributions are made both in the form of cash and in kind services. A corporation may decide, for instance, to supply musical instruments, or all the arts materials needed for a VSA Festival. And enormous contributions are made by volunteers who donate their time and talents to the state programs each year. Each state VSA program is incorporated as an independent private nonprofit organization.

The Hands-on Programs in the States

Most corporation CEO's will tell you that the best way to take the measure of a company is not by what goes on in the boardroom so much as what goes on down on the shop floor. For VSA the shop floor is the hands-on programs in the 50 states, where, so to speak, the paint meets the canvas.

Each state organization is incorporated as an independent private nonprofit organization. States are not required to adopt all of the VSA programs, but can choose those special projects it deems suitable for its disabled people and that its staff can carry out. The national VSA supplies each state organization with a computer that can be hooked into a national special education telecommunications network. State coordinators thus can exchange information with headquarters in Washington and with other state organizations around the country.

To give you an idea of how these programs function from day-to-day in delivering services, in turning VSA concepts into reality, we have chosen three at random for brief descriptions, which are excerpted from their fact sheets and annual reports:

Iowa

VSA Iowa was formed in 1977 by Jacqueline Merritt of Dubuque and Governor Robert D. Ray with the assistance of the Department of Public Instruction, the Iowa Arts Council, and VSA. It conducts 15 to 20 Arts Festivals each year.

Each year VSA Iowa serves more than 20,000 children and adults. Of these, 70 percent are children under 21; 35 percent are mentally retarded, while 55 percent are either blind, deaf or hearing impaired, have an emotional, behavioral or social disorder, or a combination of these.

During 1986 the unit mounted 17 Arts Festivals in as many towns and cities; 15 Dance/Creative Movement programs; 25 Special Projects such as signing-to-music, plays, visual arts workshops, touring exhibits, art at summer camp. They also provided 40 in-service educational art and special education teachers workshops. They topped off the year with a Governor's Conference on Very Special Arts.

In 1985-86 Iowa spent $163,000 and in 1986-87 the

budget was $198,000. In 85-86 the money came from a variety of sources: the national VSA, $23,000; foundations, 32,000; businesses 30,000; what are listed as "organizations," 30,000; the Iowa state Division of Special Education, 15,000; the Iowa Arts Council 7,000; other government grants 4,000, and the rest from miscellaneous sources. There was 1,100 in contributions from individuals.

When they totted up the number of people this money served, they came up with these numbers: 20,000 handicapped children and adults, 1,000 volunteers, 1,500 arts and special education teachers, 1,000 recreational coordinators, 250 artists and 100 agencies and organizations. And they counted 100,000 visitors to their festivals.

Wisconsin

The Wisconsin VSA enjoys a close relationship with the Wisconsin Elks Association, which lends considerable support. During 1986-87 about 2,000 volunteers helped them reach more than 6,000 persons with handicaps.

A major effort during the year was a program to educate and train a core group of 26 outstanding Wisconsin artists and teachers in special education techniques, so that they may in turn lead workshops to train other artists, teachers, service providers and recreational leaders who are interested in using the arts to educate their special students. The program was patterned after a highly successful similar effort developed by VSA- Indiana in cooperation with Dr. Arthur Harvey from Eastern Kentucky University and George Schricker, Master Artist with VSA-Indiana.

The unit put on a New Visions Dance project during the year, promulgated the Young Playwrights Project and conducted a drama program for mentally handicapped teenagers. They also put on 11 Arts Festivals during the year.

Wisconsin's Executive director, Kay Lindblade, was intrigued by what she and her staff heard during the year from volunteers, so much so that she gathered some of them together into a pamphlet. A sampling of the comments, which seem to show that people with disabilities are not the only ones who benefit from the VSA programs.

"I haven't had a more enjoyable day in a very long time. . .In the five years I have been in school, the VSA Festival has been the most fulfilling experience I've had."

". . .the participants in the Festival are very special people and I'm looking forward to next year's Festival so I can volunteer again."

". . .I hope I was able to brighten their day as much as they brightened mine."

"A well-known philanthropist said a person should be embarrassed to die if he had not made life better for at least one other human being. Very Special Arts is a wonderful vehicle for making the quality of life better for many individuals. It provides beauty, warmth, fulfillment and the thrill of creativity to people of all ages."

Louisiana

The Louisiana program is one of the most active in the country and VSA headquarters in Washington has designated it as a model for the nation. The unit takes the fostering of the arts among its disabled clients very seriously, in its literature warning educational administrators and special education teachers what does *not* constitute creative art:

"Examples of stereotypes which stifle creativity, discourage independent and expressive thinking are:

Paint-by-number, ditto sheets, loop pot holders, and objects assembled from commercially sold kits. These should be avoided in the process of preparing for arts activities in the classroom or at the festival."

The Louisiana VSA program began in 1977 as a major component of the state's already existing Arts for Exceptional Children program. Through the joint efforts of the state's Department of Education VSA office, the Louisiana Educators Association and the universities in the state, the VSA Festivals have expanded from five in 1977 to 28 in 1985 and to 42 in 1987. More than 66,000 people take part in the Festivals throughout the year.

The Louisiana VSA conducts three-week college accredited courses with practicum for regular, special and art educations teachers in the area of art for exceptional students. It also conducts a number of inservice training programs for teachers. In 1982 the staff developed a training module for Dance/Creative Movement for teachers of preschool exceptional children. VSA gave the state unit a grant to produce a videotape on the module, with accompanying manual and resource guide. The staff also has in production a series of resource manuals for teachers of exceptional students in the areas of visual arts, music, dance and the performing arts.

The unit has a traveling exhibit which draws from the more than 300 pieces of art created by exceptional children which are in the possession of the State Department of Education. The exhibit is loaned to local educational agencies, community arts centers, museums and galleries throughout the year.

VSA and Louisiana's Arts for Exceptional Children Program provide training personnel and materials for regional and local VSA Festival sites.

The Louisiana unit engages in many other programs too numerous to list here.

Special Projects

The festivals are the signature pieces of VSA. But they are not more important than all of our other activities. The festivals are like the hub of the wheel. All the special projects are on the rim and draw their strength from and are held together by the hub. Like the hub and rim, the festivals and the projects are tightly bound together. Neither can really do without the other.

New Visions Dance Project

The development of this project during 1983 in cooperation with the Alvin Ailey American Dance Theatre is described in chapter two. Ballet companies in Des Moines and Kansas City also tested the concept and helped develop the curriculum. Instructional videotapes of VSA classes and performances at the Ailey Theatre are available from VSA to assist other companies to replicate the project.

Henry Fonda Young Playwrights Project

The project is designed to encourage script-writing workshops for students aged 12 to 18 in schools across the nation. Its purpose is to give recognition to scripts by disabled *and nondisabled* young writers that dramatize aspects of disability. One or two scripts are selected each year for a production at the Kennedy Center in the spring.

The 1987 winner was David Baker, 17, of Laie, Hawaii. VSA brought him to Washington to see his work come to life on the Theater Lab stage of the Kennedy

Center. His script was chosen from a field of 110 entries. Titled *Inside Al*, the play involves two teenagers who try to meet their teacher's assignment for a "be nice to someone" project with Al, a man with cerebral palsy, as their "someone." Al is portrayed by two actors, "Al," who has cerebral palsy, and "Inside Al," who tells the audience Al's inner thoughts. One teenager, Beth, tries a superficial approach to being nice, the other, Jason, goes overboard. Neither succeeds. Beth does not understand, but Jason learns from his mistake.

In 1985 Mr. Baker won second place in a Hawaii state writing contest for a story titled *Nature's Rhyme*. He is president of the Kahuku Drama Club. Also a musician, he plays seven instruments and participates in three bands.

A special merit award was presented to Amanda Wilcox, 13, of Shawnee Mission, Kansas. She saw a scene from her work, *Our Revels Now Are Ended*, produced at the Kennedy Center. Amanda has been interested in acting and singing since she was in first grade. She has been involved in church and school choirs and musical productions, and has written prose and poetry. She has won first place in one of her school's writing contests. She wants to be a novelist.

In Amanda's play, Grandmother, a vital and spicy former actress who uses a wheelchair, visits her daughter's family. During her stay, the elderly woman strengthens her relationship with her granddaughter by coaching the girl in acting, to which her daughter and son-in-law object. After initially rejecting being moved to a nursing home, grandmother accepts the change and the challenge to teach the people in the home how to bring some vitality into their lives.

Recipient of the first playwrights award in 1984 was

Terrylene Theriot, who was then 17 and a student at the Model Secondary School for the Deaf, which is on the campus of Gallaudet University in Washington, D.C.

When she was 15, Ms. Theriot, who is profoundly deaf, acquired a pen pal, a convict in a Texas jail. She wrote to him of her frustration at being deaf and the loneliness her condition caused her. "I was angry inside," she says, "but I had no one to tell. So I told my pen pal. Because he was kept isolated in a cell I thought maybe he would understand." She felt that if she could reach him and convince him that he was not alone, then she,too, would no longer be isolated inside her deafness. They exchanged many letters. The prisoner made it clear that he shared her anger, but not her dreams. He mocked her innocent realism. Their discussions of the meaning of isolation and its consequences helped Ms. Theriot lose a good deal of the bitterness, she said, that her condition engendered in her and she gained new insights into who she was and what her place was in the world. She now says she could have remained a prisoner of her bitterness, but instead, "I chose to see a beautiful world."

The correspondence formed the basis for her play, *Imagine*. She wrote it in American Sign Language and one of her teachers at the Model School, Tim McCarty, translated it into idiomatic English. Ms. Theriot knows little slang and has to have phrases like "bag lady" explained to her. In the performance of the play at the Kennedy Center, George Segal starred as the prisoner, and Ms. Theriot was told he was a big star. She did not know who he was.

"My play is about isolation," she says. "Just because I'm deaf doesn't mean I'm isolated. Anyone can have that. Some hearing people talk all day and go home

237

and say, 'No one understands me.' Talk is not necessarily communication. People have different kinds of isolation."

The young playwright is an aspiring actress and was headlined in many shows mounted by the drama program during her high school years. She went to England to see her play produced in cooperation with the Royal Court Theatre and also toured the British Isles in a student production of *Godspell*. She also appeared in Ireland's first VSA Festival. Since receiving her Fonda award, she has appeared as a guest performer

Terrylene Theriot, who in 1984 was the first winner of the Young Playwrights Project, co-sponsored by Very Special Arts and the Dramatists Guild. Very Special Art.

on the television series, *Cagney and Lacey*. Ms Theriot now lives in Los Angeles and is pursuing a career as an actress.

Creative Writing Project

First developed in cooperation with the PEN (Poets, Essayists, Novelists) American Center, which is an international association of professional writers, writing workshops are conducted in hospitals and institutions in such cities as Boston, New York, Chicago and San Francisco. The thrust of the program is to develop self-awareness and communication skills in institutionalized disabled people and those in long-term care rehabilitation facilities. The works produced are intended as tools that educators, parents and therapists can use to gain better understanding of the needs of institutionalized disabled persons. VSA has published a selection of the work produced by patients at Goldwater Hospital in New York City as a means of increasing public awareness of the creative talents of disabled people and to provide a guide for others to replicate the program.

Artists Unlimited

This project is intended to place works by Very Special Artists in hospitals and institutions for the therapeutic and rehabilitative benefits they may bring to patients and residents. Patients can improve their hospital rooms by displaying works of art. For disabled artists, benefits include a heightened self-esteem and increased confidence in their artistic abilities through seeing their creations chosen and valued by other people. The program exemplifies the cultural contributions artists with disabilities can make to society and demonstrates how the arts can help to integrate disabled persons into their communities. Cooperating with VSA in this effort are Humana Hospitals, the largest chain of privately owned hospital in the nation, as well as other hospitals and nursing homes.

VA Hospitals Arts Workshops

This project brings all VSA activities in dance, drama, music and the visual arts to patients in VA hospitals and encourages them to participate in VSA Festivals. The program now is nationwide after being developed and tested in California, New Mexico, New York and Virginia.

Itzhak Perlman Award

An annual award is presented to a musical artist who is impaired to provide recognition and assistance with their career. The competition is open to young artists who have a disability and are between ages 10 and 21.

Each state VSA may choose from this menu of projects as many as the staff believe will benefit their local population of disabled people and which they can administer with the staff and funds they have available

For each project there are four goals:

• To encourage organizations and artists to develop arts opportunities and programs for disabled people.

• To provide technical assistance and training for people who wish to provide art programs for disabled people.

• To establish and broaden arts programming that integrates disabled and nondisabled persons.

• To make the general population aware of the benefits art programs bring for disabled people and the great lack of such programs.

Itzhak Perlman has made himself a spokesman for disabled people everywhere, especially on the issue of accessibility of public places. Christian Steiner

VSA International

In 1982, VSA joined with the Organization of American States to spread its work to Central and South America. The following year a meeting with representatives of European nations was held in Vienna, Austria and it expanded the VSA concept to the continent. Seeing that the arts programs which resulted from these meetings were successful, VSA invited to its 1984 Festival at the Kennedy Center in Washington, D.C. disabled people and specialists who work with disabled people in other countries and convoked an international seminar on the question of arts for the disabled on a worldwide basis. Attending were representatives from the Organization of American States, and countries in Asia, Africa, Europe, the Caribbean, Central and South America and from Australia. Because of the interest in the VSA concept expressed at this meeting, VSA set up an international division, which is now headed by dancer Joanne Grady of *Moonrise*. Its charge is to encourage and help other nations to replicate VSA programs. The unit is in touch with organizations in 40 countries, which already have established VSA festivals or are in the process of doing so.

In November 1985, Italy held its first Festival. It took place in Rome and was attended by about 7,000 people. Pope John Paul came and blessed the event.

Also that autumn of 1985, the Netherlands held its first VSA Festival. It was in the 12th-century town of Amersfoort, which is 25 miles Southeast of Amsterdam. One of those attending was Queen Juliana. For the Festival day in September, the mayor turned over the city hall, which the VSA people transformed into a village of art. Netherlands Television aired an hour documentary on the event.

At the Netherlands Festival a smash hit that garnered repeated ovations was *The Hummingbird*, a French theatre group from Lille. Its nembers, aged 19 to 30, are mentally retarded and used to live in institutions. Following their performance, they told the audience, "Our goal is to explore all kinds of art that make people mature, to make the public sensitive to the art that is inside people who are different, and to show that we are complete people and have something to say."

During 1987, VSA programs were launched in a number of countries. In Jamaica, a Caribbean regional office of VSA opened in February. Projects under way include drama for students who are mentally impaired and workshops and training sessions for teachers. VSA Barbados sponsored a "Week for the Disabled" in March. In Belgium, the VSA director is developing a pilot arts program for children in special education classes and will train teachers in theatre, mime, painting, sculpture, dance and puppetry. Ms. Maria de Jesus Soares, wife of the prime minister of Portugal, visited VSA's international program unit in Washington in May. She said she plans to start a VSA program in her country. In India, the VSA program was launched with a festival in New Delhi in March. Festivals also were held in France, Ireland and Panama. In time, VSA Festivals will be held in 40 countries where the American organization has established relations with similar groups.

A Measure of Success

Measuring, or even seeing the achievements or successes of an arts program for disabled people or anyone else, is notoriously difficult. When she is asked to describe a concrete example of a VSA "success," Founder Smith often cites William Britt. He is a good choice, for his case is unambiguous proof of how effective the arts can be in releasing someone from the prison of mental retardation and the hell of severe emotional disturbance.

For 30 years, Mr. Britt, now 51, was warehoused in New York State's infamous Willowbrook Institution for the Mentally Retarded. In 1974, when he was 34 he was transferred to the Margaret Chapman School in Hawthorne, New York, which is the VSA headquarters for New York State. Medical personnel there described him as hostile, antisocial and terribly frustrated. Initially he spent most of his time in solitary activities. He was easily aroused to anger and his verbal abuse of other patients and staff at such times was stifled only by a severe stutter brought on by his anger. The consensus of the staff was that his prospects were about as limited as they could be.

In an attempt to improve his ability to get along with others, soon after he was admitted to Chapman he was introduced to the school's art workshop, which provides materials and tools for drawing, painting, wood working and metal working. He worked steadily for two years, learning, calming down and producing a series of increasingly deft acrylic and oil paintings, jewelry boxes, lamps and tables. The staff was pleased, but not overly impressed by his work, and neither was Mr. Britt. He was reluctant to let others see the art he had produced.

Then in 1976, over his objections, some of his work was entered in the New York State Southern Regional Very Special Arts Festival. When they saw his work, viewers were ecstatic, liberally bestowing rave reviews on him. Mr. Britt was stunned, and for the first time began to comprehend his own worth and that of his art work. The Festival experience changed him and changed his life. Much of his frustration and anger evaporated. He became less solitary and began to work well with others.

Subsequently Mr. Britt was admitted to art classes at Westchester Community College, and became an honor student. He also helped other students and staff at the college to solve problems they encountered in their art work. In a major step forward, in 1984 Mr. Britt was able to leave his dormitory in the Chapman School to live in a community residence with five other persons.

Mr. Britt's work has been shown in many art exhibits around New York State and he now maintains his own well-equipped studio. He has received commissions for paintings and one of his work has been sold by Sotheby's in New York City. He also continues to participate in the VSA Festivals. Each year VSA publishes a calendar featuring art of people who have participated in VSA programs. Mr. Britt's painting *Sandals* was chosen for the cover of the 1986 calendar.

Following this outstanding example of the benefits participation in the arts can bring to one person, we asked VSA's operating chief Maillard to sum up his opinion of what the organization has achieved on the national arts scene.

"We've achieved two things," he responded. "We have added programs to the arts scene that didn't exist before, and we've nurtured existing programs and brought them to the attention of leaders in the field.

"But it has been a long road and it will continue to be a long road. We face a fundamental difficulty in telling the public what the arts can mean for people with disabilities. For example, no one questions whether sports are good for people. Almost everyone in America understands what participating in sports means, and the psychological and physical accomplishments involved. Americans have no doubt at all about the benefits sports bring to people, disabled or not.

"The same perception does not hold true for art. When VSA began, we didn't fully understand art's similar capabilities. That's why VSA began with young people in the schools. We needed to establish a data base to support our outreach to more people with special needs. We built that data for our first ten years, and now we have something to show the American public.

"The majority of VSA programs have been in place for more than a decade and have proven they work. More than a million people are involved—participants, parents, teachers, volunteers artists—all of whom benefit in one way or another. What we are doing now is taking the message out and asking for support—and we're getting it."

At VSA's annual national conference in March 1987, Mr. Maillard used colorful imagery to explain to the leaders of VSA state programs and others where the organization is heading:

"We've taken the locomotive and we've stoked its fire until now this train is rolling and gathering speed. Our job is not a simple, single task. We have to run locomotives on at least three different tracks—programs, public awareness and fundraising."

Ms. Smith also addressed the conference participants:

"Much has been accomplished," she said, "yet much needs to be done. All of you have recognized that there are still thousands of children, youth and adults with special needs who do not have access to programs in drama, dance, music, creative writing and visual arts."

APPENDIX ONE
VSA ADDRESSES

National Headquarters

Very Special Arts
John F. Kennedy Center for
 the Performing Arts
Washington, D.C. 20566
(202) 662-8899 (VOICE)
(202) 622-8898 (TDD)

As time passes, the addresses and telephone numbers of some of the state VSA organizations inevitably will change. The national headquarters will be happy to supply current information. They also will supply the addresses of the VSA operations overseas.

State VSA Organizations

Very Special Arts Alabama
112 20th Street North
Birmingham, AL 35290
(205) 254-5440

Very Special Arts Alaska
PO Box 773185
Eagle River, AK 99577
(907) 694-8722

Very Special Arts Arizona
3321 North Chapel
Tucson, AZ 85716
(602) 795-6502

Very Special Arts Arkansas
PO Box 55307
Little Rock, AR 72225
(501) 666-7766

Very Special Arts California
% Los Angeles County
 Office of Education
Division of Special
 Education
9300 East Imperial
 Highway
Downey, CA 90242
(213) 803-6504

Very Special Arts Colorado
1600 Sherman Street, Suite 750
Denver, CO 80203-1611
(303) 832-3161

Very Special Arts Connecticut
The Hartford Arts Center
94 Allyn St.
Hartford, CT 06103
(203) 246-0116

Very Special Arts Delaware
Willard Hall, Room 012
University of Delaware
Newark, DE 19716
(302) 451-2084

Very Special Arts District of Columbia
% Special Education Program
Trinity College
Franklin St. and Michigan Ave., N.E.
Washington, DC 20017
(202) 939-5143

Very Special Arts Florida
% Department of Art Education
123 Education Building
Florida State University
Tallahassee, FL 32306
(904) 644-5474

Very Special Arts Georgia
% Special Audiences, Inc.
1904 Monroe Drive; Suite 110
Atlanta, GA 30324
(404) 892-3645

Very Special Arts Hawaii
Box 88277
Honolulu, HI 96830-8277
(808) 735-4325

Very Special Arts Idaho
Box 8059
Idaho State University
Pocatello, ID 83209
(208) 236-3156

Very Special Arts Illinois
318 Waldman
Park Forest, IL 60466
(312) 481-6100

Very Special Arts Indiana
1605 East 86th St.
Indianapolis, IN 46240
(317) 253-5504

Very Special Arts Iowa
Department of Education
Grimes State Office Building, 3EN
Des Moines, IA 50319-0146
(515) 281-3179

Very Special Arts Kansas
No address available. Program was being reorganized as we went to press.

Very Special Arts Kentucky
366 Waller Ave., Suite 119
Lexington, KY 40504
(606) 278-4712

Very Special Arts Louisiana
2525 Wyandotte St.
Baton Rouge, LA 70805
(504) 342-0181/0182

Very Special Arts Maine
Box 8534
Portland, ME 04104
(207) 761-3861

Very Special Arts Maryland
200 West Baltimore St.
Baltimore, MD 21201-2595
(301) 659-2219

Very Special Arts
 Massachusetts
2 Boylston St., Second Floor
Boston, MA 02116
(617) 350-7713

Very Special Arts Michigan
Box 30008
Lansing, MI 48909
(517) 335-0447

Very Special Arts Minnesota
5701 Normandale Rd., Suite
 315
Minneapolis, MN 55424
(612) 922-2928

Very Special Arts
 Mississippi
Box 5365
Mississippi State, MS 39762
(601) 325-2367

Very Special Arts Missouri
Behavioral Studies
 Department
University of Missouri-St.
 Louis
8001 Natural Bridge Road
St. Louis, MO 63121
(314) 553-5752

Very Special Arts Montana
Box 8485 Hellgate Station
Missoula, MT 59807
(406) 243-4847

Very Special Arts Nebraska
% Metro Arts Council
Downtown Station Box 1077
Omaha, NE 68101
(402) 341-7910

Very Special Arts Nevada
% Sierra Arts Foundation
PO Box 2814
Reno, NV 89505
(702) 329-1324

Very Special Arts New
 Hampshire
Box 2338
Concord, NH 03301
(603) 228-4330

Very Special Arts New
 Jersey
841 Georges Road
North Brunswick, NJ 08902
(201) 745-3724, 745-3885

Very Special Arts New
 Mexico
PO Box 7784
Albuquerque, NM 87194
(505) 768-5188

Very Special Arts New York
 State
5 Bradhurst Ave.
Hawthorne, NY 10532
(914) 592-2180

Very Special Arts New York
    City
100 East 42nd St., Suite
    1850
New York, NY 10017
(212) 983-2965

Very Special Arts North
    Carolina
% Division for Exceptional
    Children
116 West Edenton St.
Raleigh, NC 27603-1712
(919) 733-3921

Very Special Arts North
    Dakota
North Dakota Dept. of
    Public Instruction
600 East Boulevard - State
    Capitol
Bismarck, ND 58505-0164
(701) 224-4525

Very Special Arts Ohio
228 Creative Arts Center
Wright State University
Dayton, OH 45435
(513) 873-2299

Very Special Arts Oklahoma
State Dept. of Education
2500 North Lincoln
    Boulevard
Oklahoma City, OK 73105
(405) 521-3034

Very Special Arts Oregon
% Oregon Education
    Department
700 Pringle Parkway S.E.
Salem, OR 97310-0290
(503) 378-3136

Very Special Arts
    Pennsylvania
% College of Arts and
    Architecture
270 Chalmers Bldg.
Pennsylvania State
    University
University Park, PA 16802
(814) 865-6570

Very Special Arts Puerto
    Rico
Suite 285
Call Box 7886
Guaynabo, PR 00657-7886
(809) 752-5620

Very Special Arts Rhode
    Island
% ARTREACH Program
Rhode Island State Council
    on the Arts
95 Cedar St., Suite 103
Providence, RI 02903
(401) 277-3880

Very Special Arts South
    Caroiina
Coastal Centers Special
    Services Coop.
Jamison Road
Ladson, SC 29456
(803) 873-5750

Very Special Arts South
    Dakota
% Black Hills Special
    Services Cooperative
181 Cliff
Deadwood, SD 57732
(605) 578-2361

Very Special Arts Tennessee
% Tennessee Department of
  Education
132 Cordell Hull Building
Nashville, TN 37219
(615) 741-7453

Very Special Arts Texas
Box 50017
Austin, TX 78763
(512) 327-6683

Very Special Arts Utah
1343 Lincoln St.
Salt Lake City, UT 84105
(801) 486-7760

Very Special Arts Vermont
% State Department of
  Education
120 State St.
Montpelier, VT 05602
(802) 828-3111

Very Special Arts Virginia
Virginia Department of
  Education
Division of Special Ed.
Box 6Q
Richmond, VA 23216
(804) 225-2883

Very Special Arts
  Washington
% Washington Alliance for
  Arts Education
158 Thomas, Suite #16
Seattle, WA 98109
(206) 441-4501

Very Special Arts West
  Virginia
% Dept. of Special Ed.
W. Va. College of Graduate
  Studies
Institute, WV 25112
(304) 768-9711

Very Special Arts Wisconsin
1045 East Dayton St.
Madison, WI 53703
(608) 255-9908

Very Special Arts Wyoming
1603 Capitol Ave., Suite 204
Cheyenne, WY 82003
(307) 634-8812

APPENDIX TWO
ARTS ORGANIZATIONS AND PUBLICATIONS

With the exception of the first two entries, the listings are organized according to the chapter in which they are described.

Jewish Guild for the Blind
15 W. 65th St.
New York, N.Y. 10023
(212) 595-2000

Distributes two-track cassettes free. Recently began putting on cassettes the monthly marketing guide for artists and craftspeople, *The Crafts Report.*

Recording for the Blind, Inc.
20 Roszel Rd.
Princeton, N.J. 08540
(800) 221-4793

Distributes four-track cassettes free. Has a number of titles on the business aspects of being an artist.

Chapter Two: Dance

The Gallaudet Dancers
Physical Education
  Department
800 Florida Ave., N.E.
Washington, DC 20002

Dance Department
Model Secondary School for
  the Deaf
800 Florida Ave., N.E.
Washington, DC 20002

National Technical Institute
  for the Deaf
Rochester Institute of
  Technology
One Lomb Memorial Drive
Box 9887
Rochester, N.Y. 14623

Anne Riordan
Department of Modern
  Dance
301 Dance Building
University of Utah
Salt lake City, Utah 84112
(801) 581-7327/3819

Videotapes Available from VSA Washington:
Dance in Silence. 1982. 30 mins. $45. Portrait of a program in which teenage dancers, with and without disabilities, form a dance company. Shows the value of the experience for youngsters.
Dubuque Dance. Dubuque Dance. 1985. 6 mins. $35. Documentation of VSA Iowa's ballet technique and movement class for handicapped students.
See the Rhythm, Feel the Dance. 1984. 30 mins. $45. A documentary of VSA Oklahoma's program in conjunction with the Oklahoma Ballet for hearing-impaired young dancers. Signed.
Special Students, Special Teacher: Anne Riordan. 1982. 25 mins. $45. A documentary of this renowned teacher's pioneering work in dance and movement with students who have disabilities.
To Feel, To Move, To Dance. 1980. 28 mins. $45. Describes methods used with children who have disabilities by Magic Movers, a professional creative movements/dramatics company affiliated with the University of Montana School of Fine Arts. Developed as a training accompaniment to an activities manual which is provided with the tape.

Booklet Available from VSA Washington, DC:
New Visions Dance Project. $4.00. An introduction to the concept. A curriculum guavailable for VSA programs and dance companies. An introductory tape may be rented for $12.00.

Chapter Four: Drama

Living Stage Theatre
  Company
6th and Maine Ave., S.W.
Washington, DC 20024
(202) 554-9066

The National Theatre of the
  Deaf
Hazel E. Stark Center
Chester, Conn. 06412

Drama Department
Gallaudet University
800 Florida Ave., N.E.
Washington, DC 20002

Drama Department
National Technical Institute
  for the Deaf
Rochester Institute of
  Technology
One Lomb Memorial Drive
Box 9887
Rochester, N.Y. 14623

Drama Department
Model Secondary School for
  the Deaf
800 Florida Ave., N.E.
Washington, DC   20002

William Rickert
Associate Dean of
  Humanities
Wright State University
Dayton, Ohio 45435

Dues for membership in the Association for Theatre and Disability are $10 a year. Membership includes a newsletter.

Not yet published, the book *Resources in Theatre and Disability* is expected to sell for about $11.

Videotapes Available from VSA, Washington, D.C.:
Climb. 1983. 10 mins. $35. Discusses theatre performance as a means of conveying skills in the classroom to students who have disabilities. Teaching concepts are described and performed.
Dracula. 1986. 10 mins. $35. Documents a VSA Iowa drama project. A high school production of *Dracula* which mainstreams students with learning disabilities into all aspects of producing and performing an all-school play.
Ready to Play. 1982. 20 mins. #35. A teacher/artist training tape depicting drama activities with young, severely handicapped children. Developed by VSA and the Getz School of Tempe, Arizona.

Chapter Five: Puppets

Kids on the Block
9385-C Gerwig Lane
Columbia, MD 21046
(800) 368-KIDS (except
  Maryland)
(301) 290-9095 (in
  Maryland)

Cost of puppets ranges from $500 to $1,000, depending on the amount of equipment -- wheelchair, crutches, braces, etc. -- that is required. One-day training sessions for up to 25 persons are $750 plus travel costs for the two KOB staff members who conduct the session.

Famous People Players
(This address is for
information only)
301 Landsdowne Ave.
Toronto, Ont.
M6K 2W5 Canada
(416) 532-1137

Mainstage Management,
Inc. (This address is for
bookings of the Players)
5520 E. Second St., Suite H
Long Beach, CA 90803
(213) 433-6771

Performances by the Players can be accompanied by workshops that have been designed for the general public, theatre students, and educators of the handicapped. Audience size may range from 20 to 250 people. Diane Dupuy leads the workshops and brings with her several performers. Topics covered are:
   * The story of the group's founding and their history.
   * Demonstration of their theatrical and lighting technique.
   * The problems of being handicapped and the joys of working with people who are disabled.
   * The vital role of discipline.
   * Integration into the community.
   * Employment.
   * Public attitudes.
   * Successful fundraising.
Cost of a Players' performance or workshop depends on a number of variables, such as the possibility of block bookings, etc., and are determined on an individual case basis.

George Latshaw designs and gives special performances with custom puppets. He also presents demonstrations and workshops and arranges residencies in puppet theater. For information:

George Latshaw Puppets
8005 Swallow Dr.
Macedonia, Ohio 44056
(216) 467-9794

In *Puppetry for Mentally Handicapped People*, Caroline Astell-Burt draws on her own experience to demonstrate how the art of puppetry can make material contributions to the lives of persons who have mental limitations, including those who are profoundly handicapped. The work covers how to invent puppets, how to make them, and how to use them to develop the imagination and enrich the experience of handicapped children.

    * ISBN 0-285-64933-7. Soft cover. 198pp. $17.95. Available from:

Brookline Books
PO Box 1046
Cambridge, MA 02238
(800) 666-BOOK

Puppetry With Students With Special Needs. 1985. 10 mins. $35. Describes a puppetry project with students with various disabilities. Developed by VSA Iowa.

Chapter Six: Visual Arts

The book *Art and Disabilities* by Florence Ludins-Katz and Elias Katz is being republished in early spring 1988. At the time this was written, the price had not yet been set by the publisher, who is:

Brookline Books
PO Box 1046
Cambridge, Ma 02238
(800) 666-BOOK

The center which Mr. and Mrs. Katz run is:

The National Institute of
   Art and Disabilities
233 South 41st St.
Richmond, CA 94804
(415) 620-0290/0299

Free catalogues of adaptive equipment for cameras are available from:

Flaghouse, Inc.
150 North MacQuestion
  Parkway
Mount Vernon, N.Y. 10550
(914) 699-1900

Photo Therapy
Milwaukee Wellness
  Resource Center
204 East Capitol Dr.
Milwaukee, WI 53212

Sherry Products, Inc.
1501 Pacific Coast Highway
Hermosa Beach, CA 90254

Porter's Camera Store, Inc.
  PO Box 628
Cedar Falls, Iowa 50612

Polaroid has a division titled Special Needs Adaptive Photography (SNAP) which produces modified cameras, wheelchair supports, special manuals. The Project Coordinator, Susan Gagnon, will accept collect calls.

SNAP
Polaroid Resource Center
784 Memorial Dr.
Cambridge, MA 02139
(617) 577-5636, Voice or
   TDD

The Vivitar company also has adaptive equipment such as flash equipment and special tripods.

Lloyd Pentecost
Customer Service
Vivitar Corporation
1630 Stewart St.
PO Box 2100
Santa Monica, CA 90406

The blueprints and instructions for building the more elaborate version of the electric drawing board with the cabinet cost about $22, including postage. Mr. Harvey estimates the cost of materials for this version at about $700. Labor costs would vary greatly, depending on who builds it. Blueprints and postage for the economy model without a cabinet cost about $12 and the cost of materials is estimated at about $300.

Mr. Harvey suggests that a technical school or vocational high school might be willing to take on construction of a board as a class project. Several of the boards have in fact been built by schools. The designer is a member of the Experimental Aircraft Association and his local chapter, in Cadillac, Michigan, has volunteered to build a board for any artist in that region.

Jack Harvey
8728 Arnold Rd.
Route 3
Manton, MI 49663
(616) 824-3430

Videotapes Available from VSA, Washington, D.C.:
A Gallery Experience for Handicapped Children. 1979. 18 mins. $35. A documentary involving children with various disabilities who tour a contemporary exhibit at the Los Angeles Junior Arts Center, examining and comprehending the displays through tactile exploration.
Another Way. 1984. 8 min. $35. Documents a VSA Iowa visual arts project in tie-dying with students experiencing behavioral disorders.

Chapter Seven: Networking

Disabled Artists' Network
PO Box 20781
New York, N.Y. 10025

Ms. Aronson stresses that since DAN has no dues, it has no treasury, so when communicating with the group it is necessary to enclose a stamped, self-addressed envelope for a reply.

Association of Handicapped
   Artists, Inc.
503 Brisbane Building
Buffalo, N.Y. 14203

The Buffalo office is the sales subsidiary of the Association of Foot & Mouth Painting Artists Worldwide and from it the work of foot and mouth painting artists may be bought. The association admits only foot or mouth painting artists to membership. Inquiries about membership or stipend awards should be made to the Buffalo office. Applicants should send three to five original works to enable the jury of the association to judge the artist's ability.

Tom Willard, Executive
    Director
Deaf Artists of America
PO Box 18190
Rochester, N.Y. 14618
(716) 244-8697, Voice, TDD

For information on the Arts Conference: Creative Endeavors Stimulate Success:

Anne Britton, Director
Center for the Disabled and
    Handicapped
Wright State University
Dayton, Ohio 45435

Chapter Eight: Poetry

Karen Chase
New York Hospital-Cornell
    Medical Center
Department of Psychiatry
Extended Treatment
    Services
21 Bloomingdale Rd.
White Plains, N.Y. 10605
(413) 637-3432

Jack Kreitzer
Black Hills Special Services
    Cooperative
Nemo Route Box 215
Deadwood, South Dakota
    57732
(605) 347-4467

Chapter Nine: Prose

The Hesperian Foundation
PO Box 1692
Palo Alto, CA 94302
(415) 327-4576

The foundation has a catalogue of publications, films, video tapes and slide programs that are for sale and for rent. Al prices include postage. Some publications are available on mi crofiche. The foundation also has an emergency field microfiche reader that allows the use of sunlight to read the microfiches

Publications:

Disabled Village Children. 670pp, 4,000 line drawings, 200 pho tos. English only. $9.00. 12 or more $7.00 ea.
Where There Is No Doctor. 464pp, many line drawings. Editions in English, Spanish, Portuguese, Khmer. $8.00 in U.S. 12 or more $6.00.
Helping Health Workers Learn, David Werner and Bill Bower 640pp, English, Spanish, Portuguese. $8.00 in U.S. 12 or more $6.00.
Describes a people-centered approach to health care and pre sents successful strategies for effective community involve ment. Slide shows 1-15 are a sampling of the topics covered.
Where There Is No Dentist, Murray Dickson. 208pp. English Portuguese. $4.50 in U.S. 24 or more $3.50.
Encourages people to take the lead in caring for their owr teeth and gums. Suggests ways to teach dental hygiene in the home and school. How to recognize and care for many commor dental problems. How to make and use inexpensive denta equipment and make temporary fillings and remove a tooth.
The Struggle for Health, David Sanders. 232pp, English only $5.50 in U.S. What must happen before health becomes a reality in a country with limited resources. Shows how the most dan gerous illnesses in the Third World today are not mysterious tropical maladies, but the same diseases that prevailed in late 19th-century England.
Project PROJIMO, 64pp, photos. English, Spanish. $3.50 in U.S

The story of the village rehabilitation in Mexico that serves disabled children and their families. The program is organized and run by disabled villagers, many of whom first came to the program for their own rehabilitation.

Where There Is No Rehab Plan, Mike Miles. 63pp, English, 3.50 in U.S.

A critique of the World Health Organization plan for community-based rehabilitation. The plan is home-based and loses the benefits of small community-run neighborhood approach. Should be studied by everyone concerned with rehabilitation strategy.

Special Education for Mentally Handicapped Pupils, Christine Miles. English. $7.00 in U.S.

Combines behaviorist and developmental approaches, based on nine years of work in Pakistan. All children can learn if we choose goals well and take appropriate steps.

Film:

Health Care by the People. 28 min. Sound, color. English, Spanish. $275 postpaid. Available for rental in U.S. only; $40. Available on videocassette for purchase only; $45 postpaid. English only. (US format-VHS-NTSC). Village health workers provide care in a rural clinic. The training of new health workers by those more experienced.

Slide Shows:

Prices include illustrated scripts in English or Spanish, and shipping by surface mail anywhere. First figure after title is number of slides.

Homemade Teaching Aids--Principles and Examples. 80. $28.
Teaching About Diarrhea and Rehydration. 72 . $25.20.
Teaching About Mothers' and Children's Health. 80. $28.
Learning Through Role Playing. 41. $14.35.
Learning to Draw and Use Pictures. 72. $25.20
Project Piaxtla: A Villager-run Health Program in Mexico. 80. 28.20.
Child-to-Child: Activities in Mexico. 65. $22.75
Family Care of Disabled Children. 30. $10.50.

Village Theatre:

Useless Medicines that Sometimes Kill. 24. $8.40
The Women Join Together to Overcome Drunkenness. 38. $13.30
Small Farmers Join Together to Overcome Exploitation. 19.
$16.65
The Importance of Breast Feeding. 18. $6.30
The Measles Monster. 25. $8.75.
How to Take Care of Your Teeth. 13. $4.55.

Magazines:

KALEIDOSCOPE
326 Locust St.
Akron, Ohio 44302
(216) 762-9755

Published twice a year, January and July. $4.00 a single copy
in U.S.; $8.00 a year. International: $6.50 and $13, U.S. cur-
rency.
   The following is taken from the magazine's information sheet
for writers:
   Audience: Disabled people, 50 percent; rehabilitation professionals 40 percent; art councils, writing and educational organizations, 10 percent.
   General Publishing Information: Considers unsolicited material; simultaneous submissions acceptable; publishes previously published work. Acknowledges receipt of MS in two
weeks. Acceptance or rejection may take up to six months. All
payments noted below are maximums, and are those prices paid
to writers and artists of established reputation. Percentage of
maximum is paid at discretion of the editors and is a relative
judgment as to the quality of the piece within the limits of the
magazine's budget. All those who are published receive contributors' copies and complimentary subscriptions. All published material is paid for; payment on publication.

   Nonfiction: articles relating to the arts; new technology if
related to art field, e.g., computer graphics; political activity,
interviews; personal accounts if art-related; biography. Inter-

ested in satire, humor. Up to $100 for a featured piece. Recent features: Man's Inhumanity to Man: A Look Inside Institutions by Burton Blatt; Frida Kahlo: Painter of Pain by Joseph L. Baird. Special assignments are made to writers who become established with the magazine.

Fiction: Up to $50 for a quality short story; 5,000 words maximum.

Poetry: Very much interested in high-quality poetry. Up to $50 for a body of work.

Book Reviews: Important works in the field. Pays up to $25.

Photographs: Usually must accompany article, but will consider on individual basis. Up to $25 a photo.

Special Tips: KALEIDOSCOPE is a serious fine-art and literary magazine which challenges readers to confront feelings about disability. We select material which projects valid roles, and hope to establish a substantive body of work in the field of disabled studies.

The Disability Rag
Subscriptions
PO Box 6453
Syracuse, N.Y. 13217

$9 a year standard rate	$15 organization rate
$6 a year tight-budget rate	$19 international rate (U.S. currency)
$12 a year generous person rate	$22 for first-class mailing

Editorial
PO Box 145
Louisville, KY 40201

Voice Indexing:

Voice Indexing for the
  Blind, Inc.
4116 St. Andrews Place
College Park, MD 20740
(301) 935-5772

Voice Indexing distributes the following publications:

Voice-Indexed Cassettes: A List of Titles Generally Available. 25pp. Free. Available in large print and on voice-indexed cassette.
Procedure for Sequential Voice Indexing on 2-track and 4-track Cassette Recorder. Free in large print. $1.00 for cassette version.
Voice Indexing Manual. $5.00. General information on voice indexing plus detailed procedures for production of tape on Sony 105 for transfer to cassette.
Selected Cassette Recorders Suitable for Sequential Voice Indexing. One-page list of 23 machines. Prices, advantages and disadvantages of each. Free.

Other V.I.B. Services:

* Informing print-handicapped persons about availability of voice-indexed cassettes.
* Developing procedures for local production of voice-indexed cassettes.
* Instructing Special Ed and rehabilitation teachers in do-it-yourself voice indexing.
* Consulting with publishers and consumers about the preparation of specific voice-indexed tapes.
* Speakers for civic groups, church groups, and service agencies about the need for access to print reference materials.

Chapter Ten: Music

Ruthlee Adler
8209 Wahly Dr.
Bethesda, MD 20817
(301) 365-2886

National Association for
    Music Therapy
505 Eleventh St., S.E.
Washington, DC 20003
(202) 543-6864

American Association for
    Music Therapy
Nadine R. Wobus
16001 Alderwood Lane
Bowie, MD 20716
(301) 249-1703

American Association for
    Music Therapy
66 Morris Ave., PO Box 359
Springfield, NJ 07081
(201) 379-1100

Canadian Association for
Music Therapy
PO Box 1208
Woodstock, Ontario
N4S 8T6 Canada

*Target on Music: Activities
to Enhance Learning
Through Music,* by
Ruthlee Adler, 1982,
169pp. $26 postpaid.
Available from:
The Glenbrook Day School
11614 Seven Locks Rd.
Rockville, MD 20854
(301) 469-0223

Charleston Conservatory of
Music and Fine Arts, Inc.
Box 113, University of
Charleston
2300 MacCorkle Ave.,
Southeast
Charleston, West Virginia
25304
(304) 344-4349

Hope University
PO Box 4818
Anaheim, CA 92803
(714) 778-4440;
714 991-8877

The Lab School
4759 Reservoir Rd., N.W.
Washington, D.C. 20007
(202) 965-6600

Books Available from VSA, Washington, D.C.:
Experiencing Music with the Piano. 1980. $4.00. A method for
teaching piano to students with mental disabilities developed
by Dr. Flora Silini, Music Professor at the University of Kansas.
Three accompanying videotapes showing children in learning
situations may be rented for $12.00.
Target on Music, by Ruthlee Adler. 1982. $25.00. Hundreds of
field-tested activities to enhance learning through music with
variations and adaptations for special populations. For therapists, teachers, parents and paraprofessionals.

Chapter Eleven: VSA

Miscellaneous Publications:
Very Special Arts Festival Program Guide. 1985. $12. A set of
nine booklets that address in detail how to solve the problems
inherent in putting on a festival. Concepts, planning suggestions, checklists, lots of nuts-and-bolts information.

Special Projects:
Artists Unlimited Project. 1986. $4.00. Details steps for bringing art work into hospitals to enhance the setting and for setting up art workshops for hospital patients.

Henry Fonda Young Playwrights Project. $4.00. Describes how to initiate a project. How to get students with and without disabilities to join together in workshops to write plays addressing an aspect of disability. Excerpts from plays that have been produced at the Kennedy Center in Washington.

An audio cassette of a National Public Radio program is for sale for $6.00. A videocassette can be rented for $12.00.

Teacher Training:
Integrative Arts Activities Guide for the Severely and Profoundly Handicapped. 1980. $25.00. A collection of 35 arts activities designed for teachers, therapists and volunteers working with persons from preschool to adult who have severe and profound disabilities.

Lite Up Your Classroom: A Manual for Burnouts. 1981. $2.00 A documentation of workshops for arts and Special Ed teachers to provide them with fresh ideas for integrating the arts into their programs. By Miriam Perrone and the staff of Camp Sunshine, Rockford, Ill.

The Arts Educator and Children with Special Needs. 1978 $3.50. A conference report on a symposium coordinated by VSA and The National Aesthetic Education Learning Center highlighting the basic issues confronting arts educators and programmers for children with disabilities.

Thumbs Up. 1984. $4.00. An arts activity curriculum guide for educators of the hearing impaired. Developed by the Iowa School for the Deaf and VSA.

General:
A Teacher's Guide for Creative Uses of American Sign Language. 1980. $2.00. An instructional guide citing new ways to use ASL in the classroom. Includes sign play, finger play, mime and Howard Seago's ASL poetry.

Directory of Theatre Programs in American Colleges and Universities for Disabled Students. 1984. $6.00. Compiled in conjunction with the American College Theatre Festival and the American Theatre Association, this is a guide to help high school students who have disabilities to choose an institution for theatre studies.

Images. 1978. $1.00. Anthology of poems by residents of the Alan Short Center, Stockton, California. Instruction by Deborah Ann Harding, poet-in-residence.

Accessibility:

Arts and Sports USA: The Professional Attractions Guide. 1984. $25. On a state-by-state listing, profiles of more than 1800 museums, theatres, stadia, zoos, gardens and historic houses. Facility accessibility, details on tours, programming, discounts, space for meetings.

The Arts and 504: A 504 Handbook for Accessible Arts Programming. 1985. $3.75. Commissioned by the Office for Special Constituencies of the National Endowment for the Arts. An overview of 504 regulations in visual, performing, media and design arts. Examines ways to make these activities accessible. Available only from the Government Printing Office, Superintendent of Documents, Washington, DC 20402. Specify stock number: 036-000-00047-3. Discount of 25 percent on orders of 100 or more.

Research:

A Review of the Published Research Literature on Arts and the Handicapped. 1971-1981. $5.00. An Illinois State University study. Organized by art form and disability; a list of dissertations on arts and the handicapped is included.

Museums:

Museum Experiences for Families with Severely Disabled Kids. 1981. $4.00. Describes a program pioneered at the Boston Children's Museum to help other cultural institutions in the preparation and planning of programs for families with severely disabled children.

Videotapes
VSA:

A Very Special Arts Story. 1985. 10 mins. $25. Narrated by Lynda Carter. VSA history, the development of Special Projects, the spirit of the programs and future directions. An excellent introduction to VSA. Open captioned version available.

Inspire: A White House Performance. 1985. 27 mins. $40. Useful for making presentations about some of the outstanding talent that has been nurtured by VSA. Narrated by Cliff Robertson.
Very Special Arts Massachusetts. 1985. 13 mins. $35. Introduces VSA Massachusetts, including volunteer orientation for VSA Festivals. Adapted from synchronized audio tape/color slide production. Open captioned.
Make a Little Magic. 1984. 11 mins. $35. An overview of the Festival at the International Council for Exceptional Children Conference in Anaheim, California.
The International Very Special Arts Festival. 1981. 8 mins. $35. Events from "Building a Rainbow Together," held during the 1981 Year of the Disabled with 500 disabled students from California and Mexico. Produced by Disney Studio in cooperation with the Orange County Department of Education.

Training for Teachers and Artists:
Access to Art: How to Begin. 1986. 26 mins. $45. For teachers, counselors and artists who wish to establish arts programs in special needs settings. Includes disability awareness, visual arts, creative dramatics, dance, and music activities. Adapted from synchronized audio tape/color slide production.
Arts and the Handicapped. 1982. In two parts, each part 60 mins. $60 for each part. Documents an in-service training session for Special Education teachers. Training ideas are provided in dance by Anne Riordan, creative play by Ed Lilley, visual arts by Scott Stoner, music by Ken Bruscia. Edited so that each art form may be used alone or the tape used in its entirety.
Arts in Healing. 1982. 30 mins. $45. Documents the New Horizons program at Children's Hospital in Washington, DC, which provides activities that contribute to the emotional growth of the hospitalized child. Features the work of a poet, a dancer, and a visual artist.
A Time Together, A Time To Share. 1982. 30 mins. $45. Produced in conjunction with VSA Wisconsin. Documents arts training of parents who have children with disabilities and examines use of the arts in the family routine.

ACKNOWLEDGMENTS

To all those whose talents, good will, grace—and sweat—we have tried to portray in these pages, our thanks for the time we demanded of them for interviews and their patient efforts to bring us to comprehend what we did not always understand when first we began to pick their brains and stir up their emotions. There are also those behind the scene who pulled on ropes and switched on lights and provided data without which this enterprise could not have come to fruition: Tracy Quinn of VSA, Paula Terry of the National Endowment for the Arts, and Ralph Schwartz, whose talents and willingness at the copy machine were invaluable. Louise Appell and Ralph Nappi read manuscript and gave good advice. Some others warrant our thanks for their willingness to serve as hand-and-head holders whenever the inevitable frustrations piled high: Bill Peterson, Kathryn Crocker and Margaret Kline. Our sons Billy and Sam and daughter-in-law Lisa had to put up with parents who seemed permanently glued to telephone, typewriter, library or computer.

A group of people who do not appear in these pages, but whose earlier efforts made the project possible deserve our thanks, and those of our readers: Representative Silvio Conte and Senators Edward Kennedy and Lowell Weicker. Without their work for the legislation, much of what we have described here would never have come to pass.

In a group of one is Kay Boyer, RN, midwife, and friend. She suggested the concept for this work and then convinced us it would serve a useful purpose.

ABOUT THE AUTHORS

Journalists for more than a quarter century, Anne and George Allen have long experience reporting on handicapped people and their problems. They also have worked with and cared for people with disabilities.

In the early sixties George studied the widespread violence which had broken out in New York City schools. His reporting revealed that unrecognized learning disabilities were a major cause of the school disturbances. To study the violence at close range George became a teacher in the city's most trouble school. His reports, which were published in the nation's largest afternoon newspaper, *The World Telegram & Sun*, and around the world, brought him one of journalism's most coveted prizes, the Heywood Broun Award, which is given to only one American journalist each year. He also received four other awards and a nomination for a Pulitzer Prize.

In 1967–68 Anne and George reported the war in Vietnam, he for ABC News, she for North American Newspaper Alliance. Anne also worked as a volunteer in a U.S. military hospital and helped care for severely disabled soldiers aboard a medical transport aircraft. After the huge 1968 Tet attack, Anne and a Vietnamese woman companion spent a week distributing rice and blankets to elderly, homeless and disabled civilians in Hue, the most heavily damaged city. In the 1987 book, *In the Combat Zone*, by Kathryn Marshall, which is about the experiences of American women in Vietnam during the war, a chapter is devoted to Anne's work.